The Style
of Paris

The Style of Paris

RENAISSANCE
ORIGINS
of the
FRENCH
ENLIGHTENMENT

GEORGE HUPPERT

*Indiana
University
Press*

BLOOMINGTON AND INDIANAPOLIS

This book is a publication of

Indiana University Press
601 North Morton Street
Bloomington, Indiana 47404-3797 USA

www.indiana.edu/~iupress

Telephone orders 800-842-6796
Fax orders 812-855-7931
Orders by email iuporder@indiana.edu

*The paper used in this publication meets the minimum
requirements of American National Standard for Information
Sciences—Permanence of Paper for Printed Library
Materials, ANSI Z39.48-1984.*

MANUFACTURED IN THE UNITED STATES OF AMERICA

Library of Congress Cataloging-in-Publication Data

Huppert, George, date
The style of Paris : Renaissance origins of the French
Enlightenment / George Huppert.
p.   cm.
Includes bibliographical references and index.
ISBN 0-253-33492-6 (cl : alk. paper). — ISBN 0-253-21274-X (pa :
alk. paper)
1. Paris (France)—Intellectual life—16th century. 2. Learning
and scholarship—France—Paris—History—16th century.
3. Philosophy, Renaissance—Influence. 4. Intellectuals—France—
Paris—History—16th century.   I. Title
DC715.H95   1999
001.2'094436—dc21   98-27645

1   2   3   4   5   04   03   02   01   00   99

*Je dy qu'il est permis à
tout homme habile et bien versé mettre
en avant ce qu'il luy semble sur tel passage et tel
autheur qu'il voudra sans le respect de l'un ou de
l'autre: car comme en une ville libre les langues
sont libres, aussi entre la République des
disciplines liberales, les iugemens
doyvent estre aussi libres.*

—Pierre Brun, *Defence* (Lyon, 1587), 63

*Mien, tien—Ce chien est à moi,
disaient ces pauvres enfants; c'est là ma
place au soleil—Voilà le commencement
et l'image de l'usurpation de
toute la terre.*

—Blaise Pascal, *Pensées*, 295

CONTENTS

The Style
of Paris

1

Portrait of a Discreet *Philosophe*

THE YEAR IS 1546. Monsieur d'Aramon, the French ambassador to the Court of the Turkish Sultan, sets out from Paris in late December, heading for Venice, where he will arrive in February to prepare for his voyage to Constantinople. This is no simple matter, since Aramon is accompanied by large quantities of baggage and by a sizeable staff which includes specialists of various sorts whom we would describe as military, cultural and scientific attachés.

Aramon, himself a military man, is experienced in matters concerning the Levant trade and Turkish diplomacy, having served both in Venice and in Constantinople previously. This new posting, however, involves a diplomatic mission of unusual scope: he is to encourage Suleiman the Magnificent to invade Hungary. In view of the mission's importance, it is not surprising that the ambassador is provided with generous resources. In Venice, he is lodged, together with his staff, in the palatial residence of the French ambassador, while arrangements are made to charter three galleys which are to carry the French party to Ragusa, the next stop on their itinerary.[1]

Among the experts in Aramon's entourage there can be found, at various times, the cartographer Nicholas de Nicolay, the topographer and archeologist Pierre Gilles, the geographer André Thevet, and the botanist Pierre Belon. These men were not on the ambassador's payroll, nor were they at his orders. The experts who accompanied Aramon were there because their own powerful patrons had arranged, informally, for them to join the expedition, perhaps at the King's suggestion, in any case with the King's approval. Gilles was in the service of the Cardinal d'Armagnac, Thevet's patron was the Cardinal de Lorraine, while Belon was a protégé of the Cardinal de Tournon, who was in the habit of surrounding himself with a phalanx of young intellectuals of very high caliber.[2]

Belon served as the Cardinal's apothecary, among other things. His instructions called for him to take advantage of the expedition to look around in the Turkish universe in a leisurely way, collecting specimens and observing whatever might be of use to European pharmacists. Upon his return to Paris almost three years later, having collected a mass of material, Belon would settle down in his Cardinal's splendid abbey of St. Germain des Prés and start writing a number of books, making good use of his field work.[3]

For the moment, Belon treated Aramon's party as a handy support network. He dropped in, both in Venice and, later, in Constantinople, when it suited him, but he felt free to go his own way for months at a time. He crossed to Ragusa in one of Aramon's galleys, but, once there, in March of 1547, he took leave from the ambassador, who was to proceed toward his destination by land, and chose to team up with another French apothecary, by the name of Villars, on an exploration of the Dalmatian coast south of Ragusa. Early spring in the Adriatic is a seductive setting and Belon was particularly interested in marine biology. There were dolphins to observe at sea and interesting flora and fauna on the islands, on Corfu, Zante, Cythera. Braving dangerous seas and escaping capture by pirates, Belon landed on Crete, which was a Venetian colony. Here he stayed for some time, investigating all sorts of things which he was to report on in his books upon his return.

It is Pierre Belon who is the subject of this portrait. His travels were to take him to "Greece, Asia, Judaea, Egypt, Arabia and other foreign countries." This was an itinerary remarkable enough for a European of his generation, although not unique, since pilgrims and merchants, not to mention apothecaries from Dijon and clock makers from Paris, come to our attention, here and there, along the way. As long as Belon stayed within the world of Italian dependencies in the Eastern Mediterranean, he was not on totally unfamiliar ground. Later, in Egypt, Syria, or the Anatolian hinterland, he would be more of an oddity, but it was not the fact that he found himself in unusual surroundings that should be most surprising to the reader of his reports. It is the author's point of view that is a revelation.

In one book in particular Belon speaks to his readers in so candid and surprising a fashion that it is possible to reconstruct something close to his philosophy from occasional and discreet clues. The book in question was first published in Paris in 1553, under the title *Les Observations de plusieurs singularitez & choses memorables trouvées en Grece, Asie, Iudée, Egypte, Arabie & autres pays estranges.*[4] Unlike Belon's other works, which are straightforward technical treatises concerning plants and animals, written in Latin for a specialized readership of natural scientists, his *Observations* are written in French and are designed to appeal to a broader audience. Even so, there were sufficient botanical and zoological data included in the book to warrant a Latin version of it.

The original French version would have appealed to readers interested in exotic travels. Belon wrote with authority about the landscape, the economy, and the social conditions of the countries he visited. He was also a writer of genuine talent. His style, bold and fresh, was a reflection of the author's stance in the culture wars of his time. He was writing his *Observations* from within a particular set of assumptions which he shared with a number of other young intellectuals in Paris. These assumptions are the subject of my inquiry.

To call on Pierre Belon as the lead witness may seem an odd way of proceeding, since Belon may be thought of as, at most, a marginal fellow traveler of the group of young men who called themselves *philosophes* and whose outlook I choose to call that of the style of Paris—*stile de Paris, modus parisiensis*—after the new and fashionable college curriculum which was at the center of their philosophical stance. It so happens that Belon the apothecary, Belon the naturalist, was also a *philosophe* with a sharp point of view on such topics as freedom of thought, social equality, and religious toleration, concerns close to the heart of writers better known to historians of literature, writers like Etienne de La Boëtie or Michel de Montaigne, who, like Belon, described themselves as *philosophes*.

Belon was a mature thinker, close to thirty years old, when he set out on his voyage, just about the time when La Boëtie, who was not quite eighteen then, could have written the first draft of his provocative diatribe against tyranny. He would have been revising it a few years later when Belon published his *Observations*. By then, the well-known botanist and the young law student would have been moving in the same circles. La Boëtie's *Voluntary Servitude*, however, was to circulate only in manuscript for another twenty years. This was how the younger Montaigne came to know of it.[5]

As for Montaigne, although he would not be ready to record his own observations on human nature for some years, he had already absorbed the lessons of the Parisian style, taught, as he had been, in the public college of the city of Bordeaux, by eminent practitioners of the style, including the young and notorious Marc Antoine Muret who, like Belon, was a member of Tournon's brain trust.[6]

The daring positions which the public might, in later years, associate with writers such as La Boëtie or Montaigne were still, in 1553, expressed mostly in private. Belon chose to publish his *Observations*, although only those familiar with the tenor of the discussions held in avant-garde Parisian salons would have been able to extricate, from the mass of botanical data contained in Belon's memoir, the ideological principles nonchalantly inserted along the way like whitewashed milestones marking the traveler's path. These markers, taken together, constitute a map which leads to a new way of seeing the world.

The very decision to write in French—to write a serious book, filled with scientific observations, in French rather than in Latin—this was already a bold departure, shocking to traditionalists. That serious poetry might be presented in the writer's native tongue, and that the result need not inevitably be inferior to the works of the Roman and Greek poets studied in the classroom—this was a point of view which had recently been expressed in print. Jacques Peletier, who had been the secretary of the bishop of Le Mans, whom Belon also served, advised poets to write in French in the introduction to his translation of the *Ars poetica* of the Roman poet Horace, published in 1545.[7] Soon after, in 1549, the poet Joachim Du Bellay published his *Deffense et illustration* of the French language, in which he restated Peletier's arguments with more panache.[8] By that time, Belon was on his way back from Greece. The Parisian literary scene into which he now settled was filled with echoes of the language debate.

In a letter written by a Parisian lawyer, Estienne Pasquier, in 1552, when he was 22 years old and belonged to more than one literary côterie, including the suburban salon of Jean Brinon, which Belon also frequented, one can hear the case being made, with great conviction, for writing scholarly and scientific works in French. Pasquier is addressing Adrien Turnèbe, the Royal Professor of Greek.

"Well, then," he writes, "you believe that it is a waste of time and a waste of good paper to write in the vernacular. You think that our language is too common to express noble ideas. If we have anything beautiful to say, you maintain, we should say it in Latin. Now, as for me, I shall always belong to the party of those who have confidence in the vernacular. I believe that we shall recreate the Golden Age once we abandon this degenerate affectation of favoring foreign things."

The Greeks, after all, Pasquier reminds his correspondent, achieved greatness by writing in their own language. The Romans, too, intimidated though they may have been by the cultural superiority of the Greeks, chose to write serious works of literature and philosophy in their own language—"and in so doing, they produced a number of *philosophes* of their own." As for the French, it stands to reason that they should study languages, not for their own sake, but as a way of gaining access to the works written in those languages. Pasquier claims to have no patience with those pedants who study Greek only to argue about some grammatical point instead of getting to the heart of what Plato or Aristotle thought. With a reformer's zeal, Pasquier conjures up a vision of the whole French nation becoming philosophical at an early age, improving in this way on previous generations, if only boys did not have to waste so many years learning Greek and Latin. "Good God," he exclaims, "don't you see how useful it would be if all worthwhile science and scholarship were available in French?"[9]

That is precisely the point of view Belon adopted. He decided to write in French and to use a simple, straightforward style, stripped of all rhetorical flourishes. The reader he has in mind is not an academic, not someone who knows much Latin, not someone who enjoys erudite digressions and debates. It is a lay audience of French readers Belon has in mind, readers who may become more knowledgeable as a result of his observations. "I wrote in French, seeking a simple form and avoiding all artifice or elegance," he explains. This choice he presents as a utilitarian one. He is concerned with "*utilité publique*" and with reaching the greatest possible number of readers so that they may share his discoveries. "Isn't it true," he asks disarmingly, "that anything worthwhile is all the more so if it is shared by the greatest number?"[10]

Belon's decision to write in French struck the academic community as so odd, so unprecedented, so undignified that the classicists among his acquaintances, searching for an explanation, suspected that his command of the Latin language was proving inadequate to the task he set himself. Denys Lambin, a young Hellenist in Tournon's entourage who knew Belon well enough and was surely envious of his success, seized the opportunity to malign him in a private letter, dismissing him as a mixer of potions who lacked a classical education.[11]

Although he obviously could write descriptions of plants and birds in Latin, it is true that Belon could express himself in French incomparably better and that, from the point of view of a classical scholar like Lambin, he was a half-baked barbarian, a rough and ready self-made man who lacked a formal education. Lambin would have been, I should think, especially prompt to detect the lack of polish in his colleague, since he was himself a young man of modest origins. Born and raised in the seaside town of Montreuil, in Picardy, he belonged to a family of locksmiths and clock makers. At the public school in Montreuil he must have shown exceptional promise and exhausted the intellectual resources available to him there by the age of 15. He continued his education in Paris, studying Greek and earning his keep by working as a servant for a wealthy family.[12]

However modest Lambin's origins were, he was already a member in good standing of the classicists' world in 1553, even before he had published anything of his own. Perhaps the same was true of Pierre Belon when he returned from the Levant in 1549. He had not published yet, but he was known as a promising botanist and as an expert on marine biology, in spite of the fact that he did not have much formal schooling. As a boy he had been apprenticed to an apothecary, and he had entered the service of the Bishop of Le Mans at about age 20. The Bishop, René Du Bellay, was a cultivated Renaissance patron on a grand scale, interested in new ideas in literature, science and religion. Rabelais was a protégé of his, and Peletier, his secretary, was an academic with broad interests in classical literature, modern poetry, and medical science, among other subjects.[13]

Belon served as the Bishop's apothecary and resident botanist and probably also as his secret agent in various missions abroad, in Germany and Switzerland, which would explain why he was encouraged to spend a year studying botany at Luther's university in Wittenberg, joining the team of students around a young and well-known professor of botany. After his return from Germany in 1542, Belon spent some time in Paris where he had the opportunity to further his studies in informal ways while working, without much success, on an eventual degree in medicine. His patron, Bishop Du Bellay, died in 1546, but by then Belon had found a new and far more influential patron in the Cardinal de Tournon. It was Tournon, for all intents and purposes the King's prime minister, who gave Belon the opportunity of joining Aramon's expedition.[14]

Just what the Cardinal expected his apothecary to achieve in the course of this voyage is hard to say. No doubt Belon was expected to bring back useful information about drugs and medicinal plants. Belon planned to collect specimens, to be sure, but he had a more ambitious objective in mind. He had started out with the intention of translating the work of the ancient Greek naturalist Dioscorides into French. It was most likely in the course of thinking about this project that he came to realize how difficult it would be to find precise French equivalents for the names of plants or animals given by the ancient author. It was Belon's intention, as he set out to explore the eastern Mediterranean shores, to establish a clear and unassailable nomenclature for the varieties of birds, fish, and plants native to the region.

Two tasks in particular awaited him in the course of his long peregrination. In the first place, he hoped to integrate exotic species, new to western Europeans, into the classifications he and his colleagues were experimenting with. In the second place, he would try to establish a reliable method for recognizing, in the flesh, through systematic observation, the species described by the ancient authorities, especially Galen and Dioscorides, whose treatises served as the foundation of formal learning in medicine and pharmacology. What he set out to do was to make sure that the words of the ancient authors actually corresponded to observable phenomena, that "les mercques escrites conviennent avec la chose qu'on descrit."[15]

This was not going to be a simple task. Feeling that he was a pioneer, Belon invokes the example of Democritus. The choice of Democritus as a model to emulate is closely linked to Belon's awareness of living in a particularly auspicious moment in human history when, after more than a thousand years of darkness, "the minds of men," which had been for so long "mired in a deep sleep" and smothered in "ancient ignorance," were at last waking up and emerging "out of the darkness in which they had been buried for so long." Rising from this noxious coma, his contemporaries were discovering every kind of knowledge. This "*renaissance*" he compares to the renewal of life in "plants which regain their strength in the warmth of the sunshine after a long, hard winter."[16]

Belon may well be the first writer to use the word "*renaissance*," in print, in French, in this specific sense. He is acutely conscious both of his debt to the admired authors of antiquity and of his own situation, as a pioneer venturing into the unknown, in the spirit of this renaissance. His voyage will be a kind of homecoming. Carrying Galen and Dioscorides in his luggage, he will retrace the steps of his illustrious mentors and he will visit the very sites graced by Homer's presence, the very sea lanes followed by Ulysses in his travels. And, like Ulysses, he is prepared to stray from his narrowly defined objective and keep his eyes wide open, "observing the diversity of customs" among men.[17]

It is as a *philosophe* that he looks at his fellow creatures. A *philosophe*, one might say, rather than a Christian. Not that these are mutually exclusive categories in Belon's mind, at least not consciously so. It is only by comparison with other Christian reporters on the Levant scene that Belon's mind-set begins to appear strangely emancipated. He invokes Democritus, not Christ. There are hardly any references in his book to God, to Christ, or to Christian worthies of any kind. Only the pagan writers of antiquity remain in the background as he stoops to harvest a plant or to observe a bird. This is a naturalist writing, after all, one is inclined to think: he can hardly turn to Scriptures or to St. Paul for confirmation of his botanical hypotheses. When the observer's eye turns from plants to human beings, however, his secular outlook frames his subjects in a way that is radically new. Reach for other descriptions of the Levant, other travel reports published by Frenchmen abroad, André Thevet's *Cosmographie du Levant*, for instance, and the distance that separates Belon from his countrymen and colleagues is instantly apparent.[18]

Thevet was only a year older. He too came from a modest milieu of apothecaries and barber-surgeons in western France, and he, too, traveled in Greece, in the Aegean, in Egypt and Palestine, at about the same time. Belon may have left for Venice and Paris by the time Thevet availed himself of Aramon's hospitality, so that the two travelers may not have met in Turkish lands, but they could hardly have avoided meeting in Paris, in the Latin Quarter, where Thevet found lodgings upon his return. Thevet's book was published in Lyon a year after Belon's *Observations* came out in Paris.

The contrast between Thevet's account and Belon's is striking for many reasons, but one of the more obvious qualities of Thevet's book is the way the author clings to a traditional Christian perspective, even though his subject is geography. "My first intention was to see the sites where the Savior first preached the news of our redemption," he tells his readers.[19] As he sets out on his travels, Thevet admits that the prospect of mingling with infidels caused him considerable concern, but "the Creator loves travelers," as can be deduced from Genesis, Exodus, and other scriptural sources. Convinced of this, Thevet embarks in Venice, on June 23, 1549, "after hearing Mass, as is proper in a true Christian," his fears held in check by his trust in God, "whom the sea and the winds must obey."[20]

What distinguishes the two men, I should point out, is not a lesser or greater level of devotion or piety, even though Thevet happens to be a Franciscan friar, albeit a reluctant one. Both men are Christians, both are interested in the ideas of the evangelical reformers, both are protégés of Cardinals, both will, as is so common in these years, pull back eventually and adopt, at least outwardly, an anti-Protestant perspective in later years.

The most telling difference between the two travelers is that Belon the scientist, the disciple of Galen, sheds all received opinions as he approaches new sights and new people, while Thevet remains entirely wrapped up in a thick compilation of old wives' tales, never lifting his eyes from the books he copies, never bothering to encounter a real person or a real animal in his travels. He might as well have stayed home.

It is hard to believe that Thevet spent some time on the island of Crete, for instance, where Belon also stayed a year or two earlier. All Thevet can think of doing is to retell a few ancient stories about Cretans and their moral character. They are "tough, arrogant and malicious," as St. Paul once noted. Needless to say, they are notorious liars and their laziness is "a sin odious to the eyes of men, abominable before God." As for their priests, they are the worst offenders, "big hypocrites, evil and depraved," even though they say they are Christians. This is, in sum, "the meanest nation and the most outrageous in their behavior toward strangers." Even the island's cattle are peculiar. It seems that the cows which graze in the environs of Cortyna suffer from an anatomical anomaly: they lack spleens.[21]

Thevet saw nothing in the course of his visit, it seems, or, if he did, he had no idea about what was worth reporting. In the end, he must have looked up references to Crete in four or five obvious and ancient reference works and paraphrased what he found there, packaging stale tales of ancient origin in such a way as to reinforce the Latin Christian reader's prejudices against Greek Orthodox priests.

When you turn to Pierre Belon's account of his visit to Crete, you enter an entirely different universe. Belon reports nothing that he has not seen with his own eyes. That is the essence of his method and that is why he invents a new form in the title of his book. *Observations*, probably used here for the first time in French, was a clinical term borrowed from Latin medical usage. Belon sets out to observe men just as he observes fish, allowing nothing to come between his trained eye and the object of his curiosity. He takes pride in the fact that he appropriates nothing from any other source (*non traduict de l'autruy*). He relies exclusively on whatever he has observed with his own eyes (*oculairement observé*).

It follows that he is not about to retell old stories or to offer sweeping condemnations of the Cretans' moral character. Neither a storyteller nor a moralist, he lands on the island with a clearly defined research program. His chief interest is in describing the flora and fauna and in tracking down whatever correspondence there may be between the nomenclature used by the ancients and modern French usage (*appelations antiques conferees avec les noms François modernes*). His second objective is to describe the customs (*moeurs*) of the islanders with the same objectivity he brings to descriptions of pelicans or arborvitae trees.

He approaches this task with what can only be described as a historical mind-set. That is to say, he does not record his observations of native speech or popular culture for their own sake, in the spirit of an ethnographer. Instead, he is always on the lookout for a vanishing past. Crete, like the rest of the Greek world, was once part of a thriving civilization, "the chief source of all the sciences and of all the learning we revere today."[22] And yet, a western scientist traveling in the Greek world now is forced to reach the conclusion "that all the Greeks now live in an astonishing condition of ignorance."[23] The question, then, which he tries to answer by means of his "ocular observations," is a historical one: how can one explain the collapse of civilization in the East?

In his attempts at answering this question, Belon keeps his eyes open for any visible or audible traces of ancient pagan culture, not so much in the form of ruins as in the *moeurs* of living Greeks, in their language, to begin with. They do speak Greek still, to be sure, but their Greek is corrupt, he observes, it is transformed by the passage of time. He establishes a distinction between the Greek spoken by the urban population which is in daily contact with Italian speakers and the Greek spoken by the inhabitants of the interior, of the countryside, who are insulated from contact with the outside world. The dialects spoken by these farmers, he believes, are more likely to have "retained something of their ancient past," as he can verify, on occasion, when he finds an ancient word still in use to describe a plant or a fish.[24]

However much the language of the people may have been eroded over the centuries, popular customs, he finds, still retain elements of their pagan origin. As he observes a Cretan funeral, he is amazed to discover a connection between ancient accounts and the rituals performed in his presence. It is as if the written page had suddenly come alive. "It is the most fantastic thing one can imagine," *c'est une chose la plus fantastique qu'il est possible de penser*, but it appears that the funeral customs of the ancient pagans survive in Greek lands. He reports on a scene which he witnessed. At dawn, he observes, the women of the village get together and begin to wail, beating their chests, scratching their faces, and pulling their hair. A professional mourner, "a woman with a good voice which is louder than those of her companions," sings the praises of the dead man, recounting his achievements from the time of his birth, while the other women continue to mortify their flesh.[25]

On a happier occasion he has the opportunity to observe a village festival while staying as the guest of a Venetian estate owner in the interior of the island. He describes the strange festivities which take place on a hot summer day. The men of the village begin dancing in the noonday heat, wearing white tunics, wide belts, and high boots. They are armed with swords and they carry bows in their hands throughout the dance which continues throughout the afternoon and into the night. Drinking hard and singing, the men perform in front of their wives and girlfriends (*amoureuses*) in what seems to be a trance-like state. Belon, observing intensely, thinks he can detect in this martial marathon the survival of a pagan custom, the *pyrrhica saltatio*, mentioned by several ancient authors as a Cretan specialty.

While he is measuring the distance between classical civilization and the current state of Greek culture, it never occurs to Belon to judge the Greeks he encounters from the perspective of a Roman Catholic, which is the common practice of other Latin travelers in the East. Instead of the opposition between Roman Catholic and Greek Orthodox or, for that matter, between Christian and infidel, Belon grasps an entirely different distinction, that which opposes "Ignorance" to "Philosophy." Heaping praise upon his patron, the Cardinal, he insists that Tournon is an "*enemy capital de l'ignorance*," picturing him as a Renaissance *philosophe* engaged in mortal combat against the defenders of "*ignorance*."[26] In the East, Belon points out, all the Greeks live "in an amazing condition of ignorance."[27] There is not a single university anywhere. There are no books to be found in Greek monasteries. The monks are illiterate for the most part. In sum, "there has not been a person of learning in all of Greece for a very long time." Since Greece, at one time, had been the very fountainhead of philosophy, of science, of letters, the question naturally arises: how was all learning extinguished over time? The hypothesis Belon proposes is not far in spirit from Edward Gibbon's formulation: the triumph of religion and barbarism. In Belon's view, so profound a cultural collapse could be explained only as the result of a concerted strategy on the part of "the prelates of the Greek Church" who are "*ennemis de la philosophie.*"[28]

What Belon is measuring is not just a deficit in literacy or book production. He is not reporting on a simple case of underdevelopment. When he speaks of ignorance, he has a particular kind of ignorance in mind,[29] and when he speaks of learning, it is a particular sort of learning he means, learning of the best sort, as his medical colleague and fellow Du Bellay protégé, master Rabelais, would have said. The monks of Mount Athos do own a handful of tattered manuscripts, but these are concerned with liturgy, not with secular learning of the kind that is still so new and exciting in the West. This new secular learning, inspired by the example of the best minds of antiquity, founded on observation and reason, free of dogma and superstition and emancipated from blind obedience to authority—this kind of learning is absent in the East. In a word, the Renaissance has not reached Greece.

The opposition between philosophy and ignorance is clear cut; it may be said to correspond to an ideological perspective; but it is not used to denigrate the "ignorant" East. The ignorance which he observes is treated as a specific historical condition. It has nothing to do with the natural intelligence of the Greeks he becomes acquainted with. Illiterate monks on Mount Athos, with whom he spends some time, possess admirable qualities, he tells us, in spite of their ignorance. The Greeks who were once supremely philosophical may shed their current ignorance again, some day. After all, was it not just yesterday that the West awoke from its "deep sleep of ignorance"?[30] And what had been the cause of that long hibernation? Belon stops short of reaching the logical conclusion that in the Latin West, as in the Greek East, it was theologians and bishops who conspired to kill philosophy.

The search for philosophy and the diagnosis of ignorance are not afterthoughts incidental to his purpose. These preoccupations are inseparable from his observation of the natural world. Wherever he lands, he begins collecting fish, birds, grasses, and resins, always with an eye to Dioscorides' and Galen's descriptions, trying to bridge the abyss which separates the last *philosophes* who had come this way, some fourteen centuries earlier, and himself, the reborn *philosophe*, stepping into territories still veiled in darkness and littered with the ruined remnants of a once-great civilization. On the Aegean islands, on the Greek mainland, in Asia Minor, in Syria and Lebanon, everywhere Belon sees impressive ruins out of the corner of his eye and hurries past, appreciative but conscious of his limitations. Archeology was the specialty of his colleague, Pierre Gilles.[31]

Belon copied the occasional inscription, admired the solidity of ancient marble walls, allowed, in passing, that "someone interested in antiquities would need more than eight days to see" the ruins of Baalbec, but he reminds the reader that these are matters outside of his area of specialization; they are "*hors de nostre observation.*"[32] Stone walls, sarcophagi, and inscriptions, however admirable, are best left to others. They are interesting to him as permanent reminders of the ancients' presence in this part of the world, but he is by nature and training better at observing living specimens.

He cannot help, occasionally, wasting time when he is persuaded to visit a famous tourist attraction. On Crete, it is the Labyrinth, of course, which is unavoidable. With ill grace, Belon inspects the site and declares it to be a simple stone quarry. In Palestine, he manages to avoid some of the standard sights on the Christian tourist circuit, unlike Chesneau, Aramon's secretary, who visits them all, reverently.[33] Occasionally, when he is confronted with one of the hard to avoid sights, presumably on the automatic circuit of the local Franciscans who acted as guides, Belon seizes the opportunity, in his notes, to debunk legends hoary with age. He reports on his visit to the river Sambatyon, near Hebron, in the Holy Land. This river had the reputation of being so reverently observant of the Lord's commands that it respected the Sabbath, flowing only on weekdays.[34] Belon makes a point of reporting that he went to see the river, observing the famously pious stream on a Sabbath, and found that it flowed as usual. "Obviously, this is a lie," *il est manifeste que cela est un mensonge*, is his conclusion.[35]

The actual location of the legendary river was in dispute. Chesneau, who covered the same ground and who reported in meticulous detail on every miraculous and sacred spot on his route, does not mention the river, which Belon places near Hebron. It is possible that the Franciscan guides showed the site to Belon and not to Chesneau, but it is also quite possible that Belon simply seized the opportunity to deliver a blow to superstition and just made up the incident. In the same breath he managed to destroy another superstition according to which Jews are given to bleeding profusely on Good Friday. "We were with them on Good Friday and we did not observe any loss of blood," he notes dryly.[36] Uncovering superstition, especially where it is linked to phenomena he is expert at observing, is one of Belon's favorite pursuits.

Belon's skepticism, ready to confront the opinions of ancient pagans or modern Christians, is especially in evidence when the test case lies squarely within his area of expertise. He may not care one bit about identifying the site of an ancient city correctly—this is the least of his worries, "*le moindre de nostre soucy,*" since ruins are man-made objects—but where Nature is concerned, he cares a great deal about verifying the exact truth. Whatever the most respected writers of antiquity may have reported, Belon goes on record and states flatly, as a result of his own observations, that there are no navigable rivers on the island of Crete. When the test case involves pharmacology,

Belon is prepared to go all out to prove the credulity not only of ordinary mortals, but of kings and philosophers as well.

A good example is provided by his investigation of the notorious *terra sigillata*, a special clay mined only on the island of Lemnos. The clay in question was one of several exotic products used as drugs and highly prized in the West, on a par with Egyptian mummy flesh: the King of France, it seems, never traveled without a supply of both mummy flesh and *terra sigillata*. Belon wanted to verify the claims made for the therapeutic virtues of the Lemnos clay. It was sold in apothecary shops in Constantinople in the form of small round tablets inscribed with Arabic characters. Belon collected samples from a number of sources and began testing the tablets, noting their coloration, texture, taste, and other qualities. This method proved generally inconclusive, except for the discovery that the tablets sold as Lemnos clay were far from uniform. Were some authentic, others not? Since the reputation of *terra sigillata*, in antiquity as in modern times, rested on its provenance, the surest way of investigating the drug was to sail for Lemnos, as Galen had done.

Belon was well aware of the ancient reputation of the Lemnos clay. Both Dioscorides and Galen had reported on it. Here was a drug known to the ancient authorities, still being produced and valued in his own time. It was a classic opportunity for establishing the concordance between ancient words and modern things. Belon found a brigantine sailing for Lemnos and reached the island, after several perilous encounters with pirates and violent storms at sea, only to discover that the clay, whose extraction was controlled as a Turkish state monopoly, could only be mined on a single day each year, the sixth of August. Already made suspicious by the lack of uniformity of the samples he carried with him, Belon naturally looked askance at a product for which special virtues were claimed only when it was harvested on a special day. This sort of thinking must have seemed to him of a piece with the tradition of the Sabbath-observing river.

Stubborn and persistent—or else stranded on Lemnos with nothing else to do—Belon kept himself busy by practicing medicine on the island and interviewing all and sundry inhabitants about the curative virtues of the island's famous clay. He interviewed Greek monks and fishermen and Turkish officials too. He put the number of his informants at 600. Unable to participate in the unearthing of the *terra lemnia*, since he could not be present on the sixth of August, he settled for a rigorous reconstruction of the annual event based on interviews and on an inspection of the site. The resulting report shows that on the appointed day a solemn procession assembles at a specially designated chapel on the way to the mining site. Mass is celebrated for the participants, who then depart for the sacred site where, once again, monks pronounce prayers before the digging starts. The clay is extracted under the vigilant supervision of Turkish officials and sent on to Constantinople in sealed leather bags.

What could be learned, especially at second hand, from this account? Nothing useful, on the face of it, unless one compared contemporary practice with what Dioscorides—and later Galen—had noted. Like Belon's own informants, Dioscorides emphasizes the importance of rituals performed before the clay may be collected. Instead of a Greek Orthodox mass, the practice noted by Dioscorides involved the ritual slaughter of a ram dedicated to the goddess Venus. The ram's blood was mixed with the clay. When Galen visited Lemnos, the rituals he observed were no longer those performed in Dioscorides' time. Galen saw a priestess pouring grain onto the clay, rather than blood. And now that Christian priests had replaced pagan priestesses, the rituals had changed once again. The principle of uniformity was violated. Did the effectiveness of the drug depend on ram's blood and Venus? Or grain? Or a Levantine mass? Or none of these? "Manifestly," writes Belon, "different ceremonies have been performed over this *terra sigillata* at different times and the clay has been marked in different ways in the course of time." This discovery leads him to observe that "trivial things of little value are made precious by means of ceremonies and things of little intrinsic worth can acquire authority when they are ennobled by superstition."[37]

Superstition, clearly, is a telltale mark of ignorance. It is the *philosophe's* duty to expose superstition wherever he encounters it, whether it is the kind of superstition that ennobles an object of no particular worth, investing it with imaginary attributes, as in the case of the Lemnos clay, or whether it is the kind of superstition that makes pious Christians abstain from eating meat in Lent.[38] Superstition is by no means the monopoly of Greek monks or Franciscan friars. Even the most rational of pagan *philosophes* could be taken in by popular traditions like that of the Lemnos clay or of the Cretan labyrinth. Reports of legendary beasts keep troubling Belon in the course of his explorations. What was the origin of the ancient belief in unicorns? Aristotle reported on an animal believed to sport a single horn, but Belon could find no evidence to corroborate the story. As for the ancient accounts of the Sphinx, Belon easily reaches the conclusion that "everything that has been written about this animal is pure fable." His proof is unassailable. It is founded on the assumption of the uniformity of Nature. Had there ever been such an animal, its appearance would have been unchanging. Yet the various artistic representations of the Sphinx, in stone or in medals, in Egypt or in Rome, are far from uniform, he concludes, after painstaking observation. The artists, it follows, could not have been working from a live model.[39]

Belon is ready to doubt the assertions of even the most respected ancient authors when the evidence of his own eyes contradicts them. He can express doubts about Herodotus, although he holds back from affirming his own conclusion and presenting it as fact, since he could not verify the ancient report from his own observation.[40] He is on solid ground, however, when he can correct the reports of ancient naturalists, as in the case of plants mistakenly identified.[41] He does not need to perform laboratory tests in order to know what to think about the ancient belief in the special powers of iris roots, which grow plentifully in the wild on Macedonian mountain slopes. According to the ancient authority Theophrastus, the root had to be harvested by a man who abstained from sexual contact. The earth around the iris root had to be irrigated for three months with sweetened water. "By such ceremonies they intended to appease the earth," writes Belon, including this example of ancient superstition among others in his catalogue of ceremonies performed to endow natural phenomena with supernatural properties.

Always ready to correct the errors of his predecessors, Belon is pleased to explain the source of their confusion.[42] Whether it is a mistaken plant identification or an erroneous account of the construction technique employed by the ancient Egyptians, Belon takes the trouble to get it right and chides those who came before him for their lack of precision. The problem is that they were not thinking correctly: *ils pensent mal.*[43] Only by correct thinking and reliable observation will the world be seen as it really is. This need to get at the demonstrable truth is an obvious asset when identifying plants.

It is also useful when the *philosophe* reaches conclusions about human beings. Just as the rational botanist must laugh off old superstitions concerning iris roots or therapeutic clay, so the rational ethnographer needs to forget fanciful tales concerning exotic peoples. Jews do not bleed on Good Friday. Nor is it likely that they require the blood of freshly slaughtered Christian children to stay alive, as legend had it.

Belon is too prudent to bring up this explosive topic, but the controversy over accusations of ritual murder was hard to miss in Wittenberg when Belon lived there. While Luther was calling for the extermination of Jews, an anonymous pamphlet attributed to Andreas Osiander provoked the ire of both Catholic and Protestant theologians eyeing a Final Solution to the Jewish problem. Osiander, an erudite and unorthodox Lutheran minister who, among other things, wrote the disarming preface to Copernicus' epoch-making book in 1543, set about debunking the old myth of ritual murder at a time when innocent men, women, and children were burned alive, accused of drinking the blood of Christian children.[44]

Belon's attitude toward those whom his colleagues referred to as infidels is remarkable. The Jews, in particular, the most despised and feared of alien peoples, are presented in his *Observations* as people whom he understands and whose qualities he is capable of admiring. Because Belon is a practicing pharmacist and physician, he falls in, as a matter of course, with Jewish pharmacists and physicians in the Turkish Levant where these professions were practiced almost exclusively by Jews. It seems likely that Belon had already established contacts with Jewish physicians in Venice, at the beginning of his expedition. In any case, he is usually to be found in the company of Jewish colleagues in the course of his travels. His interest in mining technology leads him to visit the Jewish manager of a mining operation with whom he stays as a house guest, conversing with him and gathering data.[45]

Wherever he happens to be in the Ottoman empire, where so many recently arrived Jewish technicians and entrepreneurs of Spanish, Portuguese, Italian, German or Hungarian origin were setting up shop, he notes their industriousness and the fact that they "thrive under Turkish rule."[46] In Macedonia he observes that the seaport of Cavalla, which had been ruined and deserted not long ago, was now a busy and flourishing city after the arrival of several hundred Hungarian Jews. In Palestine, he notices the terraced hillsides which testify to the industry of biblical Jews[47] and the prosperity of fishing villages newly established by Jewish pioneers.[48]

The Jewish colleagues whom he frequents are indispensable to him, since they speak "all the languages." They interpret for him, but they do more than that. There is no one else he can turn to for a knowledgeable account of the way things work in the East. His Jewish informants alone can explain the context of what he is seeing.[49] Belon's respectful attitude toward Jews is part and parcel of his attitude toward all the ethnic groups he encounters. Underlying his perspective, which is radically different from that of the other experts connected with Aramon's mission,[50] is a philosophical axiom which, as a naturalist, he takes seriously, namely the proposition that human beings are all members of the same species and are therefore all the same, just as swallows or cows are all the same, allowing only for slight variations. This general theory does not allow for cows with missing spleens, Jews who bleed on Christian holy days, or rivers that behave in strange ways. In the same way, any observable differences between Frenchmen, Turks, Greeks, Arabs, or Jews can only be explained by the different historical circumstances which shaped these nations, not by biological causes.

The Turks, for instance, whose qualities Belon admires much of the time, do suffer from some deeply ingrained flaws, but even the worst of these can be explained. It is true that Belon is left speechless when he tries to explain Turkish culinary habits. He simply cannot stomach the crude foods put in front of him and his resolve as a *philosophe* melts away at the dinner table. He is perfectly tolerant of religious differences, but where food is concerned he remains a Frenchman, making no concessions. "The great lords of Turkey eat mechanically, seeking no pleasure," he reports in disgust. "They eat their cu-

cumbers raw and they use no napkins." Their salads "are served without oil or vinegar," he adds, with genuine condescension, "for such is the custom among these unfortunates (*ces pauvres gens là*)."[51]

Turkish dietary customs, however appalling they may be, are not signs of innate depravity. Unlike Thevet or Nicolay, Belon remains consistent in his application of the Stoic-Epicurean axiom summed up by Cicero: "no single thing is so like another, so exactly its counterpart, as all of us are to one another."[52] Are the Turks reputed to be especially grasping, do Turkish officials prey upon the subject population with astonishing rapacity, even by European standards? This may well be true, as Belon's observations bear out, but the Turks' behavior can be explained.

Belon's explanation, for which he is most likely indebted to his Jewish interpreters of Levantine customs, is that the Sultan, fearing corruption, rotates his officials constantly, so that opportunities for graft are limited to a short time span in the course of which the beys and pashas squeeze out as much as they can from the local population.[53] Outweighing the less pleasant features associated with Turkish rule, there are positive advantages, even from the perspective of conquered populations. "This country has never been more prosperous" than under Turkish rule, an elderly Greek informant tells Belon.[54]

This may well be true, thinks Belon, and material well-being is not a negligible factor in human happiness. As a *philosophe* with the appetite of a social theorist, Belon is struck by the volatile nature of status distinctions in the Turkish world, so different in this respect from the hierarchical and aristocratic nature of European society. "In this country," explains Belon, "there is no point in claiming to be noble," *il ne sert de rien en ce pays là de s'avouer estre Gentilhomme.*" This is because there is nothing like a hereditary nobility in Turkish society, he discovers.[55] In a sense, all Turks are social equals since all of them are equally the Sultan's slaves. The elevation of a Christian Bosnian Serb farmer's son to the most powerful office in the empire is worth noting, although the vizier's meteoric rise says nothing about the destiny of his eventual descendants. All power is ultimately borrowed and ephemeral, granted and abrogated at the Sultan's whim. Upon his death, even the most favored of pashas may lose all the property he amassed. This is why, Belon conjectures, there are no splendid *châteaux* to be seen in the midst of the most strikingly prosperous territories under Turkish rule. Their wealth being so clearly of a transitory nature, Turkish lords do not choose to sink their money into elegant mansions.

Having made his point about the profound difference between the Turkish and European élites, Belon proceeds to theoretical considerations: "Since various societies have defined nobility in different ways," some, like the French, maintaining that it was a genetically inherent quality, others, like the Turks, viewing it as an administrative position in no way transmissible to one's heirs, it would seem to follow that "nobility is whatever one wishes it to be."[56] Since there is no observable uniformity in this matter, it follows that nobility is as fanciful a construct as the representation of the Sphinx.

Obviously inclined to embrace the natural equality of human beings as axiomatic, Belon relishes the egalitarian customs of the Turks, customs which, in his view, are closer to Nature than are the customs of Europeans. He is reminded of the contrast between Turkish and French behavior at every road-side stop. The Spartan nature of Turkish shelters for travelers is a source of amazement to him. There are no inns here, he explains, no elegant lodgings for gentlemen, no comfort, no luxury, that can be purchased. The Turkish public hostel, where travelers may spend the night, is a philanthropic foundation endowed by some wealthy person for the convenience of all who pass through, Belon reports. There is no charge for using these facilities. Everything is freely provided. Horses, mules, and camels are watered. Free soup is offered to the travelers, each of whom brings his own gear, which consists of a round leather tablecloth, drawn together like a purse, as well as a bowl and spoon. The rooms contain no furniture. They are just sheltered spaces in which travelers may settle down for the night. The remarkable thing about these arrangements that Belon finds so striking is what they reveal about the nature of Turkish society: "no Turk, whoever he may be, is in the least ashamed of lodging in such a hostel, nor is he ashamed of accepting charity." This is simply the custom of the land, *la façon de faire* of this country where "any stranger is treated exactly as would be the greatest personage." No one is turned down, "regardless of whether he is a Turk, a Christian, a Jew or an Idolater."[57]

These *façons de faire* clearly meet with Belon's approval, in part because of his philosophical convictions and, perhaps, in part also because of his own modest origins. The customs of the Turks appear to him as far more rational than those of his own countrymen. He goes out of his way to make the Turks seem like noble savages whose natural simplicity has only recently given way to more civilized behavior through their contact with educated Jews of western origin.[58]

His praise of Eastern customs extends to Greek Orthodox Christians. Instead of excoriating Greek Orthodox priests, as Thevet does, for their stubborn deviation from Latin ritual and usages, Belon adopts a neutral stance. "A number of nations in various parts of the world follow the Christian law in different ways," he observes, in the course of a visit to Mount Athos where he collects unusual plant specimens and finds the Greek monks interesting, too.

As an ardent supporter of the revival of letters, and as a *philosophe*, he is naturally distressed at the ignorance of the monks, but their ignorance, he believes, is not the monks' fault. They are forbidden, by the leaders of their Church, on pain of excommunication, to approach any sort of secular learning. While Belon naturally deplores this state of affairs, he is quick to recognize the natural talents of his hosts on the holy mountain. These monks may be illiterate, but they are never idle. While book-learning is palpably absent among them, by order of their superiors, their natural intelligence is evident in the way they choose to live.

Without actually saying so—there is no need to—Belon contrasts the way of life of the Greek religious with that of their counterparts in the West. "You will never find one who is idle," he says of the Greek monks, steering straight for the stereotype of a monk in his readers' minds. These Greek monks, far from being lazy parasites, are truly industrious, a quality Belon admires above all others. "They walk out of their houses at the crack of dawn, carrying their tools and a haversack, filled with some dry bread and onions, slung over their shoulder." Each of them works, not for himself, but for the community, some in the vineyards, others felling trees, others still, building boats. "There are tailors, masons, and carpenters among them and they all work together."[59]

Having made his point about the frugality, the industriousness, and the egalitarian habits of the East—qualities so notably absent in the West—Belon completes his account of this observed Utopia by stressing the religious toleration he finds in the Turkish empire, this being another quality notoriously absent among Europeans, as he could testify from his own experience, having been imprisoned in Calvin's Geneva for possession of Zwinglian literature.[60] "The Turks," he notes, in the course of his stay on Lemnos, "are not as zealous as the Greeks and many other nations" when it comes to affirming the superiority of their own religion over others. "They allow the Greek Christians to perform their prayers over the Lemnos clay in their presence." They even go so far as to assist the Christians in their ceremonies.[61]

Belon's friendly attitude toward infidels should have caused indignation among tradition-minded readers. Here was a Frenchman who found nothing to condemn in the customs of the Turks except their cuisine. Here was a man who did not take the nobility seriously, who showed little respect for the Christian clergy, who felt free to discount the opinions of Aristotle and to mock miracles. Yet Belon's book was a success. No censorious eyebrows greeted its publication. This may have been, in part, the result of the author's discretion. It seemed far-fetched to look for subversive ideas in a book ostensibly devoted to botanical observations. It is also true that, in 1553, Belon's way of looking at the world would not have been considered particularly odd in the Latin Quarter, among the gifted protégés of such patrons as the Cardinal de Tournon, the Cardinal de Lorraine, the late bishop Du Bellay or the chancellor Michel de l'Hospital. At court and in the bookshops there was a receptive audience for the reflections of a *philosophe* of Belon's kind, as we now shall see.

2

In Monsieur Brinon's Garden

BELON DOES NOT NAME NAMES. Hardly anywhere in his book does he tell us who his friends are, what current books he favors, where he stands, if anywhere, in the fierce ideological debates of his time. Is he an Erasmian? Does he despise the theologians of the Sorbonne? What of the vogue of skepticism ushered in with the publication of Cicero's *Academica?* What has Belon read, besides Galen and Dioscorides? Total discretion on all fronts.

He is not about to show his cards in this book dedicated to his Cardinal and written in the Cardinal's luxurious Parisian abbey of St. Germain des Prés. He does not mention his previous patron, the controversial bishop René du Bellay. No mention of Rabelais or Luther, both of whom he must have met and read. Not even that most fashionable and noisily self-promoting band of poets tinged with a superficial and glamorous paganism, Ronsard's *brigade*, who were the talk of the town in 1553, not even they are alluded to, except indirectly, by means of a dedicatory poem contributed by the author's friend Nicolas Denisot, who was a member in good standing of Ronsard's group.

So it is only the most alert of readers who would be in a position to place the botanist Pierre Belon in his intellectual milieu by means of a chance reference to the garden of Monsieur Brinon. While hiking on the slopes of the Taurus mountain range, Belon came across a natural spring. As was his habit, he tried to find an equivalent for this natural wonder that might be familiar to his French readers. In so doing, he hit upon a comparison with a spring he had observed "on the estate of Monsieur Jean Brinon," at Noisy, some six leagues outside the city limits of Paris.[1]

About Jean Brinon not a great deal is known, except that he was a wealthy magistrate whose country estate was at the disposal of the most adventurous among the Parisian avant-garde in those years, roughly between 1550 and 1553, when Belon had returned from his travels and when he was occupied with the composition of several books, including the *Observations*. Jean Brinon himself may not have published anything, but the poets, classical scholars, and scientists who frequented his garden parties were an extraordinary lot. Several of them dedicated their books to Brinon.[2] Amidst the *jeunesse dorée* which frequented Brinon's epicurean parties, mature scholars such as Jacques Peletier and Pierre Belon would have figured as senior partners in a common enterprise whose objectives were several. The young men around Ronsard, some of whom were still in their teens, wished to gain fame for themselves, both by reviving the forms of classical culture and by declaring their independence from Roman and Italian models. At another level, these agitators were engaged in what one of them described as a "war against ignorance," *une belle guerre contre l'ignorance.*[3]

How did these dashing young intellectuals come together in the first place to form a well-advertised movement? One way to answer this question is to turn to the amazing career of a distinguished gentleman scholar by the name of Lazare de Baïf. Baïf was a passionate lover of classical scholarship. He spent years in Italy, where he studied Greek with the most famous Hellenist of the time, Lascaris. Baïf corresponded, in Greek, with Guillaume Budé and, like Budé, he published monographs on esoteric topics, including ship construction and pottery in ancient Greece. He also translated Sophocles into French, including the tragedy of *Iphigénie*, published in 1549 and dedicated to Jean Brinon.[4]

Baïf, having served as the French ambassador to the Venetian Republic, returned to Paris in 1534, bringing a baby back with him, a little boy named Jean Antoine (Giovanni Antonio), about whose mother, presumably Baïf's Italian mistress, nothing is known. Jean Antoine's education, which was closely supervised by his father, makes Montaigne's well-known account of his own upbringing look trifling. Baïf, upon his return from Italy, chose to settle down with his infant son in a fine townhouse on the woodsy periphery of the Latin Quarter, close to the best-known colleges and publishing houses in the kingdom. While he busied himself with his duties as a magistrate in the *parlement*, where he was a colleague of Brinon's, the elder Baïf pursued his studies and devoted himself with a perfectionist's zeal to his son's education, of which he made a demonstration project.

He hired the most accomplished tutors conceivable to work with the boy. Charles Estienne, a classical scholar and botanist, supervised the precocious Jean Antoine's education by the time the boy was six years old. When Lazare Baïf departed on a diplomatic mission to Germany, he left his son in the care of Jacques Toussaint, the Royal Professor of Greek, and took the 16-year-old Pierre Ronsard with him as his secretary, while Charles Estienne came along as the ambassador's attending physician.

Upon his return from Germany, in 1544, Baïf took his son back and hired a new tutor for him. Jean Antoine was 12 years old by then and he had already spent four years in Professor Toussaint's home, studying Greek. Reunited with his father now, he was to study at home, under the supervision of his new tutor, Jean Dorat, a classical scholar of some distinction. Dorat was a professional academic of humble background, a man in his thirties who had no financial resources other than those he could produce from teaching and tutoring. He now was installed in Baïf's mansion to work closely with Jean Antoine, and also with Ronsard, who was 20 now and still in Baïf's service.

The sudden death of the elder Baïf, in 1547, forced Dorat to take up an academic position as principal of a totally obscure college, the Collège de Coqueret, just down the street from Baïf's house. Taking the teenage Jean Antoine with him, and young Ronsard as well, as the nucleus of a paying group of boarders he meant to tutor in his college, Dorat began to serve as the mentor of a literary movement which was soon to attract attention. Ronsard and Baïf were joined by Joachim du Bellay, a cousin of the bishop of Le Mans. Du Bellay was in his early twenties. He had studied law briefly, at the University of Poitiers, where he met Marc Antoine Muret, Montaigne's teacher, who was already a classical scholar and a poet and playwright of distinction at age 20 or thereabouts. Muret was soon to be found in Paris too, teaching and keeping up relations with Dorat's group.

Among other friends and collaborators who were not actually living in Dorat's college there was Jacques Peletier, the secretary of the bishop of Le Mans, who had known Ronsard for some time and was the first to have encouraged him to write in French. Peletier's interests included mathematics, medicine, and linguistics. Like Peletier and Belon, Nicolas Denisot came from Le Mans and he, too, experimented in several directions at once. When he was in Paris, he joined Ronsard's *brigade*. He wrote verse, but he was also an artist and a cartographer, a classical scholar and a secret agent. He spent three years in England as tutor to the children of the Seymour family, but he was back in Paris in 1549, about the time when his friend Belon returned from the Orient. Among the other young poets who were in the habit of joining the *brigade* on its outings to Brinon's garden and to public readings and performances of new plays, there was Jacques Tahureau, also from Le Mans, and several young Parisians, fresh out of college or law school, including Estienne Pasquier, who later would refer to their common campaign against "ignorance."[5]

Ignorance, as Belon and Pasquier defined it, was a rather amorphous concept. In the broadest and least controversial sense, ignorance was depicted as lack of learning, of the kind of learning passionately embraced by Renaissance intellectuals. Used in this limited sense, the word could be employed to flatter amoral and profiteering teenage cardinals by referring to them as enemies of ignorance.

In a more pointed usage, ignorance was understood to be a cherished monopoly of theologians and of dull academics whose learning, it was said, consisted of a few phrases of mangled Latin jargon with which they hoped to intimidate laymen. Ridiculed in the *Praise of Folly*, in *Gargantua*, in the *Letters of Obscure Men*, such men were not only ignorant, they were also dangerous, since, like the political imams of the Islamic world, they were always ready to denounce those who criticized them, calling for their immediate arrest and execution.

More generally, ignorance was thought to reside in the *sotte multitude*, that "many-headed beast" in Horace's often quoted phrase, the vast mob of the credulous who were moved, out of ignorance, by their worst animal instincts and manipulated at will by shrewd demagogues, usually wearing clerical garb.

Although the war waged against ignorance manifested itself on many fronts, Paris served as the testing ground and the clearing house for the party of philosophy because of the number of colleges and publishing houses established in the Latin Quarter and also because of the opportunities for financial support and the synergy which resulted from the presence of what was surely the largest concentration of students and professional academics in Europe, all crowded into a small territory within Europe's most populous city.

Almost next door to Dorat's Collège de Coqueret, there was another avantgarde school which had been established two years earlier in what had also once been a neglected and obscure college, the Collège de Presles. Under the direction of a master of arts named Pierre de la Ramée, known as Petrus Ramus in academic circles, this college was becoming preeminent as a demonstration center for the style of Paris.

Ramus had achieved notoriety in 1543 with the publication of a Latin treatise designed to destroy Aristotle's authority in the university. The theology faculty reacted swiftly to this provocation, demanding the confiscation of the book and the punishment of its author. This *cause célèbre* was brought before the king. Ramus was forbidden to teach philosophy and escaped more serious consequences only because he was a protégé of the young Cardinal de Lorraine, who had been a classmate of his at the Collège de Navarre and whose influence at the court of the elderly Francis I was second only to that of the Cardinal de Tournon.

It was in the aftermath of this skirmish in the culture wars which raged in the Latin Quarter that Ramus took over the Collège de Presles and embarked upon a brilliant career as the most successful pedagogical innovator within the University of Paris. Instead of teaching philosophy in the conventional sense, that is, in the form of commentaries on Aristotle, Ramus and his remarkable staff led their students through the works of the historians, philosophers, scientists, poets, and mathematicians of antiquity directly, without the filter of later glosses and commentaries, to seek out the essence of the sort of reasoning the pagan authors alone, in Ramus' view, had been capable of.[6]

Ramus himself taught courses on Euclid's geometry as well as on Caesar's *Gallic War*, for instance, persuaded as he was that there was only one method for reasoning correctly and that this method should be sought in the works of the best minds of the ancient world, regardless of the subject these authors had chosen to treat. "There is only one method," he insisted. "It was the method employed by Plato and Aristotle," but it is at work, also, "in Virgil and Cicero, in Homer and Demosthenes, it governs mathematical reasoning, philosophy in general and human judgment and conduct. This method was not invented by Aristotle or, for that matter, by Ramus."[7]

In Ramus' view, philosophy was a natural talent. "The very first human beings" practiced it.[8] A long line of talented thinkers, from Prometheus to Socrates and, finally, to Galen, exemplified this Greek art, according to Ramus. Galen, however, was the last and "he closed the door after him."[9] Since Ramus, like Belon, was convinced that no one had been able to reason correctly since Galen's time, his chief objective as a scholar and teacher was to set off on a treasure hunt designed to unearth the secrets of the pagan *philosophes*. Believing that he was having some success in this project, he was intent on publicizing the good news as widely as possible, not only to his students and to the university community, but to a larger audience, to the largest conceivable audience. For this purpose he engaged in a program of translation into French. He began to write in French himself and he went so far as to devise a new method for spelling French words phonetically, so as to remove every conceivable obstacle in the path of those who wanted to learn to think without much formal preparation.[10]

Ramus was immensely successful, in spite of the venomous opposition of the theologians. His close association with the distinguished publishing firm of Wechel, which had published Erasmus, and whose shop was conveniently situated a stone's throw from his college, led to an unending stream of books produced at amazing speed. Many of these were textbooks intended for classroom use. These served the expanding market for editions of the *optimi auctores*, the best authors of antiquity, who were the mainstay of the Parisian style. Most of these editions could be described as unremarkable, inasmuch as they were not first editions and inasmuch as they were editions of standard authors.

The academic book market was national, even international, in scope, supplying hundreds of local schools and colleges which followed the Parisian model. As the field marshal of the war against ignorance, Ramus headed a supremely efficient team which involved not only his colleagues, his advanced students, and his publisher but cooperating scholars of all sorts, including the group around Dorat. Ramus' own effectiveness and output were doubled, to begin with, by the collaboration of his roommate and alter ego, Omer Talon, to the point where it is difficult to assign authorship at times, as in the case of Talon's publication of Cicero's *Academica* and related commentaries.[11] Among other forceful and brilliant teachers on his staff, Ramus could count on the young Provençal mathematician, Jean Péna, whom he managed to get appointed to a Royal Professorship in Mathematics at the age of 23. Péna, who knew Greek and who was among the earliest to lean toward a Copernican view of the universe, died at the age of 26, in 1558.[12]

Ramus enlisted his students in his war against ignorance. Seventeen-year-old Michel de Castelnau—the future French ambassador to England who was to shelter the fugitive Giordano Bruno in his embassy—was put to work, in 1559, translating Ramus' new book about the ancient Gauls into French, so as to make it available to a larger audience. Ramus had prepared a course of lectures that year on Julius Caesar's commentaries on the Gallic War. These lectures, in Latin, were delivered in his college. They served, among other things, as an initiation into Caesar's style, grammar, and vocabulary. The course also was intended to increase the students' knowledge of Roman history and geography.

It was no accident that Ramus chose to comment on Caesar's campaigns in Gaul. Ultimately, he intended to use the text as far more than a linguistic exercise. As an excursion into philosophical history, Caesar's testimony would serve to learn something about the ancestors of the French, the conquered Gauls who left no records of their own and whose *moeurs* could be reconstructed only from the hostile or indifferent account of the victorious Roman general. The Latin original of Ramus' treatise was published simultaneously with Castelnau's French version, both by Wechel.[13]

In his efforts at reaching beyond the confines of the university, Ramus produced a short textbook, in French, on how to think straight, under the title of *Dialectique*, in 1555. This may have been the first philosophical treatise written in French. The author's decision to publish an academic treatise in French was very much in tune with Joachim Du Bellay's manifesto of 1549 in which the poet argued that "philosophy, which was long ago and famously introduced on the soil of Attica" would flourish once again if it were transplanted "now onto French soil." Ramus' disciple, Pasquier, was at home both in Ramus' college, from which he had graduated, and in Ronsard's literary club. In 1552, in his letter to Turnèbe, Pasquier had already rehearsed the arguments in favor of using the vernacular language for scholarly publications. Three years later, with the publication of Ramus' *Dialectique*, the collaboration between the Collège de Presles and Dorat's poets at Coqueret was made even clearer, since Ramus chose to commission French translations of Roman poetry, to be used as examples in his book, from Ronsard, Du Bellay, Denisot and Pasquier, among others.[14]

On the subject of language, the young aesthetes in Dorat's college and the embattled radical in his Collège de Presles were of one mind. Du Bellay's first published poem, in 1547, had already spelled out his commitment to his mother tongue: "I write in my mother tongue and I try to improve it," he wrote, "so as to make it eternal, just as the ancients did with theirs." In the same vein, Ramus writes simply: "I love my country," and Pasquier: "I write for my France."[15] To espouse such a position in the debate over the uses of the vernacular was not necessarily perceived as a subversive move, although it was a controversial one within the academic community, especially when it was presented, in Ramus' writings, as a militant act in favor of the disenfranchised masses excluded from the university.

Ramus was well protected, however. His patron, Charles de Guise, Cardinal of Lorraine, had been elevated to this ecclesiastical dignity in 1547 at the age of 22, not, of course, because of any particular religious vocation, but because his family was one of the most powerful in the kingdom. It is hard to say which of the two cardinals, Lorraine or Tournon, was building the larger empire of properties and clients. Charles was appointed archbishop of Reims at the age of 13. A cardinal at 22, he was also, among other things, bishop of Metz and abbot of Cluny, Fécamp, and Marmoutier. His brother Louis, also a cardinal, had been named bishop of Troyes at 18 and abbot of St. Victor shortly afterwards. These ecclesiastical benefices were among the most glamorous and lucrative in France. In the sort of monopoly game played by teenage *grands seigneurs*, these properties were the equivalents of Boardwalk and Park Place.

Backed by patrons like the Guises and Tournon, the young writers who met in Brinon's garden had little to fear, it would seem. There were, however, truly dangerous currents flowing just below the surface. The chief enemy of the *philosophes* was the theology faculty, the Sorbonne, as it was known, whose power to censure and to accuse was particularly explosive in those years. There was a fault line running right through the Latin Quarter, threatening to split the university apart—and the kingdom with it. The issue was heresy, a highly contagious condition known to flourish within the universities.

John Calvin, Calvinus, as he was known in academic circles, had been a student, right at the top of the Montagne Ste. Genevieve, where all the colleges stood, only a few years earlier. His own teacher, Mathurin Cordier, left

Paris as early as 1529 to assume the low-profile position of principal at the municipal school of the city of Nevers, several hours' ride from the epicenter of troubles. Calvin fled Paris five years later.

In the forties and fifties, while Brinon's parties were celebrated in epicurean verse, and while the circle around Lazare de Baïf and Jean Dorat was occupied with translations of Sophocles and Euripides, Calvin was busy organizing the militant cadres of French Protestantism in Geneva. He too was intent upon producing a French vernacular culture, but not a secular one. It was the Bible that was to be made French, as well as the prayer books and the theological commentaries, which were rolling off the Genevan presses of exiled French printers like Robert Estienne, whose brother Charles remained in Baïf's service.

A cold wind was blowing steadily down the Montagne Ste. Geneviève, all the way down to the Rue des Carmes and the Place Maubert, at the bottom of the hill, almost at the river's edge, where Ramus' college was located, near the executioner's square where printers, booksellers, and teachers were burned alive on the recommendation of the Sorbonne.

Ramus had already experienced the wrath of the Sorbonne. In spite of the Cardinal's protection, which brought him his appointment to the Royal Professorship of Philosophy in 1551, he had been denounced more than once as a dangerous radical. This was more than a war of words. Several attempts on his life were made. His library was vandalized. He had to escape from Paris for a time, when the religious war heated up after the death of Henri II in 1559. Ramus did eventually declare for the Protestant party, although in a lukewarm way that was not entirely acceptable to the Calvinist Church.

In the early years of Henri II's reign, the tensions which would eventually explode and claim so many victims were still contained, muted, not always openly expressed. Unspoken suspicions of heresy, rumors, private vendettas disguised as ideological righteousness—all those were held in suspense in a volatile and dangerous mix. Dissent could quickly be branded as heresy. Ramus was known as a devastating critic of Aristotle and, hence, of the scholastic establishment that swore by Aristotle's authority, at a time when the most profound mysteries of the Christian faith had somehow become inextricably linked to Aristotle's metaphysics. The doubts which Ramus expressed about the infallibility of Aristotle's *dicta*, as interpreted by the Sorbonne, were perceived as mortal blows struck against the very foundations of morality and faith.

Was Ramus dangerous because he refused to accept the corpus of Aristotle's works as the unquestioned source of all knowledge? Was he dangerous because his teaching deviated from the traditional curriculum, because he redefined the meaning of philosophy? Or was he dangerous because his dismissal of traditional views, his cavalier attitude toward received ideas, could only lead to heresy? These multiple suspicions harbored by his more conservative colleagues are hard to disentangle.

Many years later, in 1572, when he was killed in the aftermath of the organized massacre of suspected Protestants on St. Bartholomew's Eve, it would still be difficult to point to the source of the hatred Ramus inspired in some quarters. The murderers were identified as non-academic employees of the university. Who sent them? The wave of executions and lynchings had already subsided when the thugs entered Ramus' chapel. Was this a contract killing? Pasquier, who was well informed, concluded that it was Ramus' rival, Professor Charpentier, who had instigated the attack in revenge for past slights inflicted upon him by his illustrious colleague.

However muted these murderous tensions may still have been in the fifties, one had to step cautiously. As long as one managed to avoid suspicions of heresy, there was no reason why the censors of the theology faculty should look closely at one's published writings. Belon's comments on Muslim, Jewish, or Greek Orthodox customs set off no alarms, even though his occasional remarks about superstitions, including the practice of fasting during Lent, might have led to trouble for the author in other circumstances. Presumably it never occurred to anyone in the theology faculty to look for heretical opinions in a book concerned with plants. Perhaps for similar reasons some of the more daring philosophical dialogues published by members of Ronsard's circle failed to invite the scrutiny of the Sorbonne.

Judging from Pasquier's experience, this was not really a surprising state of affairs. His historical researches, which he began publishing in 1560, were to attract the attention of hostile critics, who discovered deeply subversive ideas in his books only posthumously, more than half a century after he had begun publishing. In the same way, it would seem that the radical implications of the salon literature linked to Ronsard's and Brinon's circles were not immediately obvious. For one thing, the censors had their hands full, in the early fifties, with Calvinist tracts. For another, theological and philosophical works were supposed to be composed in Latin by academics. It took some readjustment to look for trouble in amusing dialogues written in French by young men with no advanced degrees. This was the category into which the dialogues written by Jacques Tahureau or Louis Le Caron fitted most obviously. Reading them, one can imagine overhearing actual conversations along the banks of the Seine, in Brinon's garden or in that of Le Caron's uncle, Valton, another wealthy magistrate.

"I do believe I hear someone in this garden who is saying all sorts of remarkably contemptuous things about mankind," says the straight man in Tahureau's First Dialogue.[16] "Aha! I see him, over there, walking about with a book in his hand," he adds.

The solitary reader turns out to be a disciple of Democritus who will be only too happy to initiate the attentive listener into his philosophy, thereby achieving his *déniaisement*, removing, that is, his naïve outlook and turning him into a critical thinker.

What is so attractive about becoming a disciple of Democritus? Well, explains the veteran *philosophe*, the chief pleasure he derives from philosophy is that he is freed "of an infinity of illusions and foolish opinions by which the mass of mankind is entrapped," including the common belief in portents, in divination, in astrological calculations. As for himself, he is lucky to belong to that small company of men who are equipped with good sense (*bon esprit*) and he seeks the acquaintance, exclusively, of other reasonable men.[17]

A certain level of snobbism appears to be the inevitable consequence of his philosophy, since reasoning correctly is a skill which is unfortunately practiced only by the happy few. In principle, nothing stands in the way of anyone achieving that most desirable state, but in practice, it has been a very long time since the bulk of mankind knew how to reason correctly. This being so, our *philosophe* maintains that he would rather "speak well and believe rightly in the company of a single person *de bon esprit*, than go astray in the company of a great number of ignorant people."[18]

Why is it that most men appear to be asleep, why do they join that "many-headed beast," the great multitude of the ignorant? Because they rely on custom, on received ideas, instead of trusting reason alone. When mankind was in its infancy, still close to Nature, men knew how to reason instinctively. Fearing attacks from "other animals," they banded together and created strong communities founded on equal justice for all and brotherly affection for each other. "Where is that natural tenderness and pity now?" asks the impassioned *philosophe*. Nature's order has been perverted, monstrous, unnatural cruelty has replaced the good judgment of instinctively rational beings—the world is now a theater of war in which the strong dominate the weak.[19]

"But," protests the naïve listener, "God would not permit injustice."

Oh, wouldn't he just, replies the *philosophe*. "Just look at Scripture. It is full of examples of virtuous men destroyed and of evil ones triumphant."[20] Overwhelmed by the *philosophe*'s argument, the listener, whose confidence in mankind is now shaken, becomes a willing disciple.

"I will wake you from a long and deep sleep," promises his mentor, who is now prepared to reveal the method by means of which his disciple will escape from "the mud pit in which the majority of men are trapped" and lead him to "the straight and beautiful path taken by so few."

The secret is contained in the teaching of Democritus. It consists of mocking everything.

"Teach me to mock," says the disciple. "What is mockery?"

"The way to mock is to show appropriate contempt for a stupid thing, while expressing this contempt in a reasoned manner and with good grace. Make no mistake," adds the *philosophe*, "this is not an easy thing to do. Only someone whose mind is quite free and unburdened with ignorance and presumption can do this successfully."[21]

The heart of the matter, for a man of *bon esprit*, is to learn to discover the truth.[22] To do this one has to go against the opinions of that "great popular beast," that mob of ordinary beings who will believe anything. Religions were invented to awe mankind into submission. The naïve mass of men, *le simple populaire*, have always been held in thrall "by a gang of charlatans whose objective it is to control men by inspiring fear in them on the pretext of their superstitious religion." Strong words, these, but hardly original, inasmuch as they echo Cicero, especially in the dialogue entitled *De natura deorum*, a standard text for students in Ramus' college and in other schools following the Parisian style. Tahureau makes a stab in the direction of exempting the religion of the Christians from his wholesale condemnation, but he does this in a halfhearted way. The grammatical structure of the sentence he adds as a disclaimer is so clumsy, perhaps deliberately, that it reads: "all those false religions (except ours) are pure inventions."[23]

The overall impression left in the reader's mind by this wordy dialogue is that the author's unequivocal endorsement of pure reason as the sole arbiter in making choices in one's life would be hard to reconcile with Christian theology. Needless to say, reason as Tahureau defines it has nothing in common with the logical argumentation which is the stock in trade of the Sorbonne, of those "*sillogisateurs d'argumens cornus*," those "dung infested masters of arts" and "aristotelian loudmouths" whom it is standard procedure to ridicule in the manner of Erasmus and Rabelais.

When Tahureau speaks of Reason, he means something altogether different and far more elusive. Like Belon, like Ramus, he considers man's ability to reason a natural gift available to all. This natural talent, in his view, has been almost destroyed by the obscurantist party led by the founders of religions. Now truly radical measures must be taken if that most valuable of Nature's gifts is to be salvaged. Those happy few who are still rational enough to mock false beliefs and who acknowledge no authority other than that of Reason must find a way to rescue "the dumb and inconstant masses" and force them to act virtuously since they lack those qualities which are found in "honest and good minds."[24] In his demonstration of the effectiveness of Democritean mockery, the *philosophe* takes on several broad categories of vain and pernicious professions, in the manner of the *Praise of Folly*, including lawyers, physicians, and aristocrats ("*Pour leur richesse et braverie en sont ils de meilleur esprit? Rien moins*"),[25] not to mention that *canaille* which quotes Aristotle, blabbing (*caquetans*) endlessly, in "a thousand dumb digressions" teeming with superfluous and ridiculous words.[26]

As for himself, the *philosophe* rejects not only Aristotle but all other authorities. Is he not an admirer of the ancient *philosophes*, then, asks the perplexed novice? Of course not, he is told. Pythagoras was silly, and so were Aristotle and Plato. What about Democritus, then? Well, even he did some silly things: he gave away his fortune, for instance. That was not reasonable. But, all things considered, with all his faults, it would be hard to think of a philosopher more admirable than Democritus.

Systematic mockery—a critical spirit, we would say—is the basic instrument a *philosophe* must learn to wield. The *moeurs* of men, the opinions of the philosophers, the dogmas of theologians, all must be subjected to pitiless scrutiny. This is a dangerous business. The *philosophe*, the man of *bon esprit*, having discovered the truth, must learn to be discreet. Broadcasting his discovery could have serious consequences for him.[27] It would be sheer, ill-considered folly to run such risks. Better to remain quiet, and even to lie, if need be, rather than endanger oneself, advises the *philosophe*, citing, approvingly, the story of a man accused of atheism who replied that he would gladly subscribe to the dogma of the Trinity to avoid being burned alive. If that is what it takes, he would subscribe to the concept of a Quaternity.[28] The dialogue concludes with the disciple's successful enlightenment. "You have removed a dark cloud which obstructed my vision," confesses the disciple. "You made me discover a clear sunlight."[29]

Reading these dialogues of Tahureau's is hardly a pleasurable experience. The more remarkable positions which he stakes out and which I have highlighted are buried in a mass of wordy and pretentious posturing. This is a young man writing, I should say, a young man of no exceptional talent, who has dutifully absorbed his lessons. Cicero, Horace, Lucretius, Diogenes Laertius, all pass in review, and Ecclesiastes too, for whom, it seems, Tahureau had a great deal of admiration.

The sources of Tahureau's "mockery" are exactly the same as those cited by Montaigne. The effect, however, is different. There is little reflection at work here and there are echoes throughout of the *badinage* in Brinon's garden, seasoning the pronouncements, making them appear less serious. Tahureau was in Paris in 1553 when he wrote these dialogues. He wrote rather hurriedly, I should think. He was getting married. He may not have intended the manuscript for publication. He had published some poems already, dedicated to the Cardinal de Lorraine's brother Louis. Tahureau was 25 years old at the time and closely connected to Ronsard's circle. Ronsard includes him, that year, in his *troupe*. In one of those promotional poems which were the common coin of the Parisian literary scene, Ronsard makes a list of his companions: "Baïf, Denisot, Tahureau, Mesme, Du Parc, Bellai, Dorat," and Tahureau does not fail to return the compliment by praising Ronsard as "*nostre premier autheur lyrique françoys.*"[30] Not that Tahureau was a supplicant in need of favors. He was the son of a magistrate from Le Mans and related to the very wealthy Tiercelin family on his mother's side. Independently wealthy and well educated, he was a young man of leisure who knew his own mind to the point of marrying a girl of absolutely no social standing.

Did he intend to publish the dialogues? Had he published them, they might have benefited from some editing but some of the freer, more provocative comments might have been excised. As it happens, he died suddenly at the age of 27. The dialogues reached print posthumously, some 10 years later. The surprising thing is their popularity. Max Gauna, the erudite editor of the dialogues, counts 17 editions between 1565 and 1602. After that, complete obscurity. Presumably, the daring Rabelaisian sallies and the references to a number of favored classical authors were appreciated by readers formed in the same mold, that of the style of Paris.

This is not to imply that Tahureau is an interesting writer. He is tiresome, undisciplined, and banal. His style is awkward when compared to Belon's sober narrative or to the natural flow of Pasquier's writing. These dialogues have worth only as testimony, as direct eye-witness testimony to the uncensored enormities which were the ordinary fare in Brinon's garden and in other private settings where *philosophes* talked freely.

There is no point in trying to pin someone like Tahureau down and to invest his loose talk with a coherence that isn't there. Is he a hidden atheist, as Max Gauna believes?[31] A rationalist, a fideist, a skeptic, an Epicurean? He may be all those things at once—and none of them too seriously. What he does, what his friends all seem to do, is to try ideas on for size, like children playing dress-up in front of a mirror. That one could face torture and execution for holding some of these ideas happens to be a fact. More to the point, I think, is that the sum of these ideas takes on a certain shape which we recognize.

In spite of his high jinks, Tahureau makes an excellent witness. Several times, in the course of the imaginary conversations he records, we find him returning to the notion that there is one idea to be grasped, an idea that is difficult to describe, a sort of wishful thinking, quite revolutionary in its essence. The gist of it is that men live atrocious lives, wrapped in ignorance and vice, when they could easily reform by returning to the kind of life Nature intended them to follow. One need not be a saint or a professional philosopher—one of those contemplative old Greeks with flowing grey beards and a predilection for living in barrels—to be eligible for the higher life. Instead, he implies, all human beings, who are by nature all the same, should aspire to this exceptional state, the only one that makes life worth living.

To what extent, one is entitled to ask, do tirades entrusted to a manuscript constitute reliable evidence about what was actually said in Brinon's garden and in the other meeting places frequented by fashionable poets? A partial answer to this question comes to us from another set of philosophical dialogues composed by Louis Le Caron who was 19 years old in 1553 and a fairly typical participant in these playful debates.[32] Unlike Tahureau, Le Caron actually saw to the publication of his dialogues. Less concerned with discretion than some of his friends, he chose to feature real people in these didactic little plays, people such as Ronsard and Pasquier, for instance. His dialogues are no more remarkable for their originality than those of Tahureau. They too make for tiresome reading. In both cases, however—and this is what matters—the youthful writers can be counted on to relay to their readers all the commonplaces they heard in the course of their association with more illustrious colleagues.

Commonplaces? Let us say that these had once, a very long time ago, counted as commonplaces among cultivated Greeks and Romans. Let loose in the gardens and classrooms of Paris now, these commonplaces acquired an air of profound subversion. They were collected from the pages of Cicero's works, they could also be found in the writings of Horace, for instance, who, like Cicero, had studied in Greece. Should the opinions of Epicurean or Skeptic writers be taken seriously—that is to say, should they be applied to modern life? Or were they to be appreciated only as an intriguing anthology of historical documents? The question hangs in the air whenever one reads the works of the youthful campaigners in the war against ignorance. This is true not only of genuinely astounding writings, but of rather banal occasional pieces such as Le Caron's.

Le Caron states his position vis-à-vis the ancients in the preface to his *Dialogues*. He "will tell you what the ancients knew and what they did not know." As for himself, says the author, he is not "a servile admirer of antiquity, nor is he so arrogant as to make light of the ancients' opinions."[33] Such a declaration of independence, in 1556, is what one would expect from a young man linked to Ramus' school. Predictably enough, he explains that his motive for writing is "*le bien public.*"

Unlike Tahureau, Le Caron is writing for publication and he presents himself as a conventional Christian. He is conventional in most other respects as well. The participants in his insufferably long-winded discussions move about in pastoral settings. They walk about in the shade of the royal gardens at Fontainebleau and they debate earnestly in the gardens of the author's uncle, in suburban St. Denis. The things they say to each other, with great courtesy, are naturally those they have learned while reading the assigned classical authors. Le Caron, whose education seems to have paralleled that of his much admired friend, Pasquier, is a reader of Plato rather than of the more skeptically inclined philosophers.

Speaking in his own name, instead of using a fanciful pseudonym, the author deplores the lack of seriousness of his contemporaries and their predilection for elegant rhetorical flourishes. He intends to dispense with such frivolities and opt, instead, for a sober and unaffected way of speaking, out of respect for *la chose publique*—the Republic, the Commonwealth—for which he feels a pure and sincere love.

The philosophical issue at the core of his dialogues is the same one we encountered in Tahureau's writings, the very same idea which permeates the writings of Ramus and is implied in Belon's *Observations*. It is expressed in the form of a heartfelt complaint: Reason no longer governs the minds of men as it once did.

Le Caron makes his case by evoking an idyllic past when men were not motivated by greed, when they were all equally rich, free, and noble. They held all goods in common, no hedges marked the limits of their fields, the very words Mine and Thine (*Mien et Tien*) had not yet been heard. These reasonable ancestors were not slaves to their possessions, nor did they think of themselves as belonging to competing nations or kingdoms. The earth belonged to all and they were citizens of the world.[34]

This natural state, when all were equal, free and reasonable, was followed, eventually, by a long period in which men, intoxicated by ignorance, fell into a deep sleep from which it is the *philosophe*'s duty to wake them. He has his work cut out for him, considering the dead weight of the "dumb masses." Engaged, together with his friends and other *bons esprits*, in the war against ignorance, Le Caron is not at all sure that he knows how victory can be achieved. He is not a theorist, not a "*contemplatif philosophe*." Much as he admires the ancients, he does not believe that one can—or that one should even try to—imitate them. This would be naïve, it would be like a game played by children who like to dress up in their parents' clothes.[35]

There is no simple prescription for reform. One cannot return to the past. However admirable the constitution of the Athenians may have been, it cannot serve as a model for a future Republic, because "the diversity of human actions is such that a single and unchanging constitution will not work. Laws have to be modified according to changing circumstances."[36] The "*diversité des moeurs*" that Belon observed in the course of his voyages could also be observed without leaving one's library, by studying the historical record.

Both methods, when employed by a *philosophe* determined to get at the truth, produce the same result. True enough, each step along the arduous path taken by the *philosophes* was a struggle. It was a narrow path they chose to follow, inestimable in the rewards it offered, but open only to a select few who had learned to reject superstition and distance themselves from the *sotte multitude* which remained stuck in the mud pits of ignorance.

Once engaged in their heroic experiment and initiated into the ways of true philosophy, converts would feel that they were waking from a deep sleep, their eyes opening, at last, to see the world as it really is. The clear light of day would chase away the last remnants of that long hibernation induced by poor thinking and encouraged by the enemies of philosophy. In this new, clear light, irrational customs would be discarded and ancient authority discredited. There was no reason to grant special privileges to the nobility for instance, no reason to swear by Aristotle, no reason to condemn the religious beliefs of anyone.

These were some of the views expressed in the dialogues of Tahureau and Le Caron. Embedded, more discreetly, in Belon's travel book, they were held by so many graduates of the Parisian style that one could easily forget how dangerous it was to express them.

3

A School for Scandal

AT THE HEART of the philosophical movement in the 1550s was that peculiar institution, the Collège de Presles, and its famous principal, Petrus Ramus, whose enemies were provoked to the point of conspiring to murder him, and whose friends were to remember him long after he was killed as a genuinely great man, a revolutionary on a par with Copernicus.[1]

The trajectory which propelled the boy Pierre La Ramée from a charcoal-burner's cottage in a village in Picardy to a Royal Chair of Philosophy is not easy to reconstitute. A key factor, most likely, was the accident of the boy's having an uncle who lived in Paris. This was also the circumstance which facilitated another notorious youth's progress from Picardy to the Latin Quarter: John Calvin had an uncle who was a blacksmith in Paris. La Ramée's uncle was an unsuccessful carpenter.

Somehow, Pierre, who was prodigiously gifted and ambitious, followed lessons in Latin grammar at the Collège de Navarre, earning his keep, it seems, as a servant, and befriending the likes of Charles de Guise, the future Cardinal de Lorraine. Although he was a student at what was then the most socially prestigious of the colleges within the University of Paris, Ramus found the experience dispiriting. Renaissance learning had failed, as yet, to penetrate the college, judging from Ramus' reminiscences, in which he describes his disappointment at having earned a master's degree, at considerable effort and after years of study, only to discover that he was "uncomfortable in his own mind." Had he actually learned anything of value? No, he concluded, "all these academic exercises had brought me nothing at all, they were nothing but a waste of time."[2]

This would have been in 1536. There he was, the penniless orphaned son of a peasant from Picardy, set free in the tortuous streets of the Latin Quarter, licensed to teach now, but convinced that he had learned nothing, that all he knew was what his teachers knew, that is to say, to "blabber on about the rules of logic."[3] In this despondent mood, he tells us, as he was walking along, at loose ends, going nowhere, "he was led, as if by some good angel," to discover the writings of Xenophon and, soon after, those of Plato. In this way, he came "to know the philosophy of Socrates."[4]

Just how this came about there is no point in asking, though one thing is clear: the dialogues of Plato were not part of the old-style curriculum. Their discovery by a young master of arts in 1536, whether it is to be taken literally or not, serves to underline the contrast between the scholastic logicians' conception of philosophy and that of the humanist writers who followed Erasmus' lead. While the stronghold of the traditionalists, in Paris, was located in the quasi-clerical world of the classroom, the new humanist culture reigned in the bookshops and in the publishers' houses where Plato, Galen, Euclid, and the other *auctores* recently rescued from their centuries-long hibernation were displayed in all their glory, in serried rows, Greek text and Latin translation, side by side.

For some seven years, La Ramée, the new master of arts, must have gone through an intensive program of reeducation, teaching himself Greek and reading voraciously. By 1543 he was ready to take on his erstwhile masters, who were still babbling on about the rules of logic, presumably, and swearing by Aristotle: he published his *Remarks against Aristotle*, which created a furor. Undaunted by the ferocious censure of the university establishment, Pierre, now a published Latin author, began to make his mark in the academic world under the name of Petrus Ramus.

He took over an empty shell of a student boarding house near the Place Maubert and moved in as principal, joined in this venture by his close friend, Omer Talon, who was also the son of peasants from Picardy. Ramus created a new college, starting from scratch, hiring a teacher of classical Greek and the inspired young mathematician Péna as well as another master of arts, the future lawyer, Amariton, whom Antoine Loisel, who spent five years as a student in Ramus' college, remembers as a teacher "who approached philosophy in a rather new way, interpreting it by means of Horace's *Epistles*."[5] In effect, Ramus established a bridgehead within the hostile territory of the university for the humanist culture which had already triumphed in the bookshops and which had already taken passionate amateurs like Lazare de Baïf by storm.

The new style of teaching in Ramus' college provoked a flurry of rumors. What was it that the university's rector heard about the subversive experiments conducted by Professor Ramus? Why, it was said that pagan Lucretius was on the reading list!

"I have the impression that you are vomiting pus and poison," wrote the rector, Pierre Galland, in a pamphlet designed to crush Ramus' reputation. Lucretius, Galland pointed out, was a materialist, an atheist "who removes all Divine Providence from this world and who considers religion and the fear of

God as among the worst evils that afflict mankind" and who, furthermore, among a host of other far-fetched and unchristian suggestions, "admits the possible existence of an infinite number of worlds." Is this the author "you choose to explain to children?" asks Galland in his prosecutorial summation?[6]

Actually, there was worse, as Galland seems to have known. Cicero's *De natura deorum* was also on the program at Ramus' school. This dialogue was described by Galland, not inaccurately, as a "skeptic, impious and sacrilegious book." Even Pliny's *Natural History*, a less controversial work, was not to be trusted in its raw state, in Galland's view, as it was bound to raise uncomfortable questions in innocent minds "unless it was commented on by a most learned professor who is, at the same time, a man of profound faith."[7]

Rector Galland's position was no longer tenable in 1551, the year in which Ramus was appointed to the Royal Chair of Philosophy and Eloquence. Galland was not an ignorant man. In spite of the venomous *ad hominem* attacks he published against Ramus, he would eventually learn to get along with his brilliant colleague. The fact is that the university's last ditch rally against Renaissance learning was collapsing. It was no longer possible to surround Plato's or Cicero's more provocative writings with a *cordon sanitaire* of interdicts and vituperations.

The printing press had opened breaches of staggering proportions in the previously closed world of the classroom. In 1536 one could still graduate with a master's degree, after completing three obligatory years of philosophical study, and conclude that one had learned nothing of consequence. By 1543 Ramus did not shrink from mounting a wholesale assault on the Aristotelian system. Two years later he set up shop in his college. By 1551, the enthusiasm for Greek studies had spread to Dorat's college, up the street, and to the Collège de Boncourt, which was turning out competent Hellenists and precocious poets such as Jodelle and Belleau, who were ready to join Ronsard's *brigade*.[8] To claim, at this point, that Cicero or Lucretius were purveyors of unauthorized substances, whose works must not be permitted in the classroom, was closing the barn after the horses had escaped.

Renaissance culture was a fashion making its way, unstoppable, favored by princes and influential patrons. It was more than a fashion, as Galland probably understood quite well. The demand for the new learning came, not from would-be priests, but from young men destined for secular careers. What could the old university, dominated as it was by theologians, offer this new kind of student? Outside of Paris, several French universities had already been made over to accommodate the new clientele. Bordeaux eliminated the old Faculties almost twenty years earlier to the benefit of a new humanities college "in the style of Paris." The city of Nîmes, which lacked a university, lobbied at Court to establish one. This was duly authorized. The city then proceeded to bypass the medieval components of a university altogether, dispensing with theology and law faculties, and establishing a purely humanist college.

Even small towns with populations of barely two or three thousand did not hesitate to establish new colleges, *stile de Paris*, in which Greek and mathematics were taught by men like Muret. Given this general trend, of national scope, feverish in the speed with which it grew,[9] how could one think of outlawing Lucretius, Cicero, Pliny, or Lucian? All the best authors—the *optimi auctores*—were pagans who harbored ideas potentially dangerous to Christian pupils, according to Galland. Yet without the *optimi auctores*, there was no education. The problem would remain insoluble until Tournon turned to the Jesuits, a few years later, relying on them to keep the subversive implications of classical texts under control, somehow.

Ramus, meanwhile, was achieving genuine fame. He seems to have been a largely humorless, driven man whose motto was, appropriately enough, "*labor omnia vincit.*" He must have gotten along on very little sleep, studying at night and preparing lectures whose eloquence was said to be truly exceptional. He kept turning out new books and he was, at the same time, so heavily involved in his college's life that he not only directed school plays but acted as a prompter and even as leading man on occasion. He found time to play handball two or three times weekly and he had a social life as well, meeting with colleagues such as the mathematician Oronce Finé at dinner time. His circle of friends included physicians, lawyers, and even theologians. He also kept up close relations with his alumni, many of whom went on to successful careers as lawyers and government officials. Two of them, Loisel and Berger, acted as the executors of his will. We owe much of this information to Nicolas Nancel, a student of Ramus' who lived for some twenty years in the college, first as a scholarship student, then as Ramus' assistant. He taught Greek and Latin and acted as the principal's secretary as well as his biographer. Eventually, Nancel was to earn a medical degree and practice medicine in Soissons and Tours.[10]

Ramus' efforts were in large part given over to making his college a successful venture within the university—and a profitable one, too. His work as a teacher and administrator, however, seems inseparable from his conviction that he was entrusted with a broader mission, that of bringing enlightenment to the university as a whole and to his compatriots in general.

"The arts and sciences had languished in a barbaric condition," within the university, until King Francis began to "bring the study of the humanities back to life," writes Ramus, in his brief for the reform of the university. He granted that progress had in fact been made, over a period of some twenty years, in making genuine learning available, at last, to the students, but a main obstacle still stood in the way of those who could not pay the tuition fees exacted from them.

Here Ramus is struggling against the medieval customs of the university that still prevailed in most of the Parisian colleges. Students were expected to attach themselves to a tutor of their choice and stay with him exclusively, for the rest of their student years, paying whatever fees he chose to ask. Outside of Paris this system had been largely abandoned to make way for what was paradoxically termed the "style of Paris," the new system that depended on graduated classes, taught by different instructors, all of whom were paid salaries.[11] This was the innovation Ramus had introduced in his own college and which he tried to introduce in the other colleges of the University of Paris. In this he failed.

He kept worrying about the "mass of good minds capable of understanding the sciences," who were left out "because they do not know Latin and Greek."[12] In his view, it was scandalous "to close off the path leading to the knowledge of philosophy to those who were too poor to pay tuition even though they were intelligent."[13] As long as the pseudo-learning dispensed in university classrooms had been largely useless, the problem may not have been an acute one, but now that authentic learning was making its way into the once-dark recesses of the university, the time had come to open up access to gifted students who, because of their humble family background, were in no position to take advantage of what was being offered.

The cost of tuition was not the only obstacle. There was the language problem, too—the custom, that is, of using Latin as the language of instruction. With this in mind, Ramus broke with tradition in a dramatic way by lecturing in French when he was appointed to the Royal Chair of Philosophy in 1551. Dorat, who had to wait another five years before he was similarly honored, complained, in Latin, about the scandalous manner in which Ramus was undermining the honor that had been bestowed upon him, by teaching in French.[14]

The lectures of the Royal Professors were open to the public. Established in 1532, these lectures continue to be offered today at the Collège de France, the modern incarnation of the institution created by King Francis I, who had hoped to entice Erasmus himself to join a galaxy of humanist scholars. Then as now, one has to admit that these lectures could not be expected to reach a mass audience. By speaking in French, Ramus signaled his intention of reaching a non-academic audience. His next step in the direction of adult education was to publish his French *Dialectique*, which contained a summary account of his teaching method and which could be considered a do-it-yourself course in how to overcome poor thinking.

What Ramus means by philosophy is exactly what Tahureau or Belon meant by it, but the *Dialectique* is not a playful dialogue, nor is the author's approach oblique. The book is a frontal attack, expressed in blunt and rather awkward French, against the forces of darkness. In the dedication, which he addresses to his patron, the Cardinal de Lorraine, the author expresses his gratitude to the Cardinal, who rescued him from the concerted assault of the "aristotelians," and goes right on to challenge his enemies in the university, who claim to teach philosophy.

Having experienced their teaching at first hand, he knew where he stood. He dismisses their learning as false, since it was not founded on reason and experience. They call themselves disciples of Aristotle, but they are mistaken. Instead of examining and testing Aristotle's precepts, as he himself examined and tested the precepts of his predecessors, these schoolmasters cling to Aristotle's opinions, religiously, without ever asking themselves whether these precepts were true in the first place and whether they were useful.[15] His own approach, Ramus explains, is entirely different. He would never rely on the opinions and on the authority of any philosopher. He relies on reason and experience alone.

For this strategy he could summon ample support from the most respected of the ancient authors. Had not Cicero advised would-be philosophers to show less regard for authority and to rely on reason instead?[16] Ramus' closest ally, Talon, had recently published an epoch-making introduction to Cicero's *Academica posteriora*, in which he defended Ramus (*meus frater*) against the dogmatists who stood in the way of free inquiry.[17]

Cicero's exposition of skeptical philosophy was presented and commented by Talon in an unprecedented way. He may well have been the first since antiquity to understand Cicero's ideas.[18] Tahureau's dialogue reflects the serious and ground-breaking scholarship of Talon—assuming that it was Talon rather than his *frater* who wrote the commentary. After the publication of Talon's work, the rumored presence, in the Paris of the 1550s, of a secret group of neo-skeptics had become a serious enough concern that Théodore de Bèze, Calvin's second in command, found it necessary to fire a warning shot out of Geneva, *Against the Sect of the New Academics*, linking this nefarious movement to the subversive writings of Sebastien Chateillon (Castellio).[19]

Were Ramus and Talon conspiring to destroy the foundations of Christian civilization? Professor Galland was convinced of this.[20] Talon had written in favor of openness and courtesy in scholarly discussion. At issue was the underlying problem of authority. Talon proposed Cicero's dialogues as a model, dialogues in which opposing points of view were stated with great courtesy and in which the speakers made no attempt to convert others to their point of view. This way of proceeding provided a sharp contrast with the dogmatic teaching methods favored by rector Galland and his colleagues.

"You will say that a student should be credulous," writes Talon. "I say he should not be credulous in studying philosophy. Would you wish to impose your own opinions on your students? Would you forbid them to seek a cause or reason for the opinions you hold? That is the way to turn your student into a slave . . . who lacks his own power of discrimination." "The last thing you want to do in your teaching," asserts Talon, "is to hand down a body of learning to be swallowed whole, without questioning, by the boys. On the contrary, you want to strengthen their own abilities and their own power to judge."[21]

Talon and Ramus knew perfectly well, of course, that Galland and his colleagues wanted no such thing, that they were incensed at the incitement to criticism and at the denigration of authority which Talon and Ramus advocated. Talon adopted the Skeptics' point of view summed up in the advice to "submit to no one's laws, in matters of philosophy."[22] Freed from reliance on other men's opinions, the *philosophes* out of Ramus' school would refrain from asserting their own conclusions. They would remain humble in the face of uncertainty and they would remain courteous toward those with whom they disagreed. This is the method Tahureau was to describe as Democritean mockery. In 1550, in an academic commentary written in Latin, such a blunt rejection of dogma and authority was perceived as a direct attack on the Christian university. What was at stake, concluded the beleaguered opposition, was all authority, not merely academic authority. "There were men in France," warned Galland, who were dead set against "all authority and prepared to introduce unlimited innovations."[23]

This was certainly one way of understanding Ramus' objectives. From the point of view of someone like Galland, who benefited very nicely from his clerical sinecures, Ramus sounded like a revolutionary ready to topple the comfortable arrangements of his colleagues. Ramus did, in fact, advocate the confiscation of clerical incomes of the kind Galland was profiting from. "Such an action," wrote Ramus, not without sarcasm, "will turn out to be a divine act of beneficence toward those opulent men who live idly." With their subsidies gone, these parasites would have to work for a living and thus be less likely to sink into vice.[24]

Although Ramus was ostensibly concerned only with the reform of the university, his opponents detected the marks of a broader conspiracy in his writings. "Who can oppose Aristotle without declaring war against our forefathers," exclaimed Galland, weighing the full implications of Ramus' philosophy which he considered "an open declaration of war against the most religious pontiffs, the most venerable emperors, the most esteemed kings."[25]

If Ramus was concerned only with academic reforms, why did he choose to offer public lectures in the vernacular? Why did he compose a philosophical treatise in French? Why publish a grammar for beginners, why invent a phonetic spelling system designed to promote general literacy in French? Since when did university men show concern for the needs of ordinary people who knew no Latin—and even for the mass of illiterates? What exactly did Ramus hope to achieve by promoting universal literacy?

His sole aim, he would reply, was to be useful. He repeated this so often that he acquired the derisive nickname of *usuarius*, "the utilitarian." His entire philosophy appeared to be founded on the desire to be useful to his fellow human beings. The purpose of learning was not that "*sotte sophisterye*," that empty grammarians' debate which was mistaken for logic in the university. Instead, the real purpose of learning was "to turn on the light of logic" (*allumer ceste lumiere de Logique*) in the minds of *bons-esprits* who desire to know the truth.[26]

Ramus' assault on Aristotle was at the center of his critics' preoccupation. Even luminaries of the humanist coterie took a position against Ramus on this issue. And not only in Paris did Ramus face a solid wall of opposition on this score. In 1569, when his presence in Paris, not for the first time, had become too dangerous for him, Ramus took a year's sabbatical to visit Swiss and German universities. By then he had opted for the Protestant cause. He tried to get a teaching post in a Protestant university and was turned down in Strasburg, even for a junior post. "Dr. P. Ramus offered his services," reads the laconic record of this episode. His offer was rejected on the ground that he was "*kein Aristotelicus*." In Heidelberg, even though he had the prince's backing and a following among the students, he was prevented from speaking and was turned down for an appointment by the faculty because he was "opposed to the truth and doctrine of Aristotle." Ramus still had hopes for a position in Geneva. In December 1570, Théodore de Bèze, Calvin's successor, dashed these hopes in a single letter. There was no vacant post, he explained. The budget was very tight. And further, "we are resolved to follow Aristotle, without deviating even in one line—I tell you this frankly."[27]

Back in Paris, twenty years earlier, Galland had understood the implications of Ramus' *Remarks on Aristotle*. Ramus's position was that the works attributed to Aristotle, whatever their merit, should not be considered the repository of the one method that could reveal all that was worth knowing. For Ramus, Aristotle was one philosopher among others. Great philosophers had come before Aristotle and great philosophers had followed. Since the beginning of the Christian era, there had been no philosophers at all, but the capacity to philosophize had not been exhausted by Aristotle—or by the ancients in general. Ramus did not think of philosophy as a science invented and perfected by Aristotle. Instead, he saw philosophy as a natural talent common to all human beings.

"The earliest men practiced it," explains Ramus. Which "earliest men"? Does he mean Adam, Cain, and Abel? I think not. "Prometheus," he tells us, "was a master of this art." Prometheus was followed, notably, by Heraclitus, Democritus, Hippocrates, Protagoras, and Zeno. Socrates, of course, occupies a very special place in Ramus's account of the history of philosophy—but this history, in his view, ends abruptly in the second century of the Christian era: Galen "was the last in line . . . and he closed the door after him so completely that it was not reopened since."[28]

How does one go about reopening this door? The answer is obvious to Ramus. The ability to reason correctly had been lost because all worthwhile literature had been lost in the general debacle of the Middle Ages. Now that the ancient authors—the reasonable authors—had been restored, the Dark Ages were over and a new light could shine upon mankind. Equipped with skills that had been lost for so long (the ability to understand Greek texts in particular), in possession of a new and growing library of classical texts, the task begun long ago in Athens could be resumed at last. And there was every reason to think that philosophy would now reach new heights, that the moderns would improve upon the ancients.

This optimistic prediction follows from Ramus's definition of philosophy. Since philosophy, for Ramus, is not a method invented and brought to perfection by Aristotle but a natural talent that can be cultivated by any person, a talent that had lain dormant for a thousand years for historical reasons, a talent that was now about to be reawakened, again, for historical reasons, why couldn't one improve upon the ancients? Aristotle, after all, had not achieved perfection in his reasoning: "Only God Almighty is a perfect logician, he alone . . . uses reason perfectly," insists Ramus.[29] Philosophy is not a technical discipline that can be pursued only by following Aristotle's logic. On the contrary, "we are all of us provided with the means for inventing everything" ("*nous avons tous les moyens d'inventer toutes choses*").[30]

If every man can reason for himself, what is there in this world that cannot be reexamined from scratch? The prerogatives of popes, emperors, and kings derive their legitimacy, after all, from the sanction of the theology faculty, which, in turn, founded its authority on Aristotle and Scripture. Ramus's position could appear more seditious than Luther's, since Luther did not question the authority of Moses and Ramus challenged the authority of Aristotle.

Not that Ramus was very much concerned with Aristotle, it seems, in his teaching at the Collège de Presles. Of Ramus's teaching, Galland observes: "He holds that philosophy is far better taught from poets than from philosophers" and "teaches no Aristotle, no philosophy, but pretty much poetry alone."[31] Galland was well informed about the teaching practices of Ramus and of Ramus's associates. The poems of the Romans were presented in the classrooms of the Collège de Presles as samples of good reasoning about the human condition.[32] This may not have made any sense to Galland, but it was perfectly consistent with Ramus's notion of philosophy.

We already have heard Ramus explain that his purpose was to learn how to reason and that good examples of reasoning could be found in Vergil and Cicero, as well as in Plato and Aristotle. No need to limit one's inquiries to philosophers: the best minds of Greece and Rome, whether they expressed themselves in prose, poetry, or geometry, were all legitimate sources to be examined in the search for "the natural laws of reasoning." This, after all, was Ramus's explicit goal: "to look for the natural laws of reasoning in the master-pieces of the human mind."[33]

In this spirit, he gave a course on Euclid after he was forbidden to teach philosophy. Why not? Was it not his contention that geometry or poetry, any activity of the human mind, could furnish him with the evidence he needed? In any case, one thing was clear: these laws, these natural laws of reasoning, had been only partially, imperfectly discovered by the ancients. The best of them—Euclid, Horace, Plato—each in his own way had made signal contributions to this search. Ramus encouraged his students to collect these valuable insights, these ancient aperçus, so as to constitute a museum of philosophical artifacts from which they could learn. The best discoveries of the ancients had to be assimilated as a first step in a modern education. It was useful to imitate the ancients and to try to equal them in one's own inventions. Eventually, one should try to surpass the ancients, to go beyond their best inventions: at that point, it would become possible to examine every-thing anew, "to do really original thinking, without even referring to the an-cients at all"—"*traiter de toutes choses par soy mesme et sans plus avoir regard à leurs disputes.*"[34]

This is the position Ramus had reached by the time he published his philosophy textbook in French, in 1555. He had come a long way since his discovery of Socrates some twenty years earlier. He had started out by declar-ing the medieval disputations a waste of time. Now he was looking forward to the day when even the ancient philosophical debates might become obso-lete. At first he had used Cicero against Aristotle. Soon he was to discover in Cicero, especially in Cicero's account of the Skeptic philosophies, a way of liberating himself even from Cicero's tutelage.

According to his exasperated critics, Ramus was doubly guilty, both of teaching impious authors and of failing to inspire in his students the appro-priate reverence for these same, damnable, authors. In spite of appearances, a kind of logic emerges: teaching pagan authors, particularly authors such as Lucretius, Pliny, and Cicero, is dangerous but inevitable. Teaching these texts as examples of good latinity is reasonably safe. Grammar is a technical discipline; philology is not necessarily concerned with ideas. As long as the humanities teacher deals with words only, with syntax, vocabulary, and style, he may be able to avoid giving his students ideas.

But did Ramus keep literature safely segregated from philosophy—philosophy, which he was expressly forbidden to teach? When he lectured on Horace, did he stick to style? No, he deduced philosophical principles—what he was pleased to call philosophical principles—from Horace's verse, from Cicero's letters. He was not training his students to compose good Latin prose; he was training them to think. And to think dangerously, perversely, irreverently, impertinently. His was a school of arrogance that had to be closed down.

In this spirit, the new rector descended upon Ramus's school, documented the accusations against his teaching practice—that he was teaching poetry in a philosophy course—and, this being against the statutes of the university, ruled that all grades and degrees issued by the Collège de Presles were henceforth invalid. Ramus appealed the ruling in court and won his case.[35] In the same year, 1551, Ramus's patron, the Cardinal of Lorraine, moved the king to appoint Ramus to a chair, a regius professorship. He was free to proceed with his "socratizing," as he put it.[36]

He had mastered the classical authors. He had dissected their works in his search for the natural laws of reasoning. He was now ready to declare his independence from the ancients. He admired their best inventions, he was sure that nothing comparable could be found in the course of the long, deadly interval since the Fall of Rome, but he was also keenly aware of the distance that separated a living Frenchman from a dead Roman. The world was different from what it had been in Cicero's time—irreconcilably different. And Ramus was not an antiquarian. He lived in the present and looked to the future.

At the beginning of his academic career he had forced his way into the magic circle of humanist culture—Budé's world, Erasmus's world. At what cost! This orphaned son of a peasant had taught himself Latin, even Greek and mathematics. What a long and arduous road he had traveled. Ramus saw as a tremendous waste the path that required students to devote the best years of their lives to mastering the ancient languages, before they could begin to think for themselves: "If the time we now spend learning these languages could be invested, instead, directly in the pursuit of knowledge," we would be able to produce Platos and Aristotles in our time.[37]

As soon as he identified the problem, he reached for its solution: he would write in French now, he would challenge others to write in French. And if the language was not ready as a medium for philosophical writing, he would get to work and improve it. His mind was already turning impatiently from the ritual genuflections in the direction of Athens and Rome that were the essence of Renaissance humanism. He was on his way to a new destination— the future. Beyond the walls of his classroom, beyond the university, there was, he believed, "a mass of good minds capable of understanding the sciences but prevented from doing so because all learning, so far, has been presented in foreign languages."[38]

Greek and Latin, as far as he was concerned, were foreign languages. Ramus's lucidity was uncommon among the classics teachers of his generation, most of whom thought of Rome as the fatherland of their imagination.[39] Since the days when Petrarch had begun conversing with the illustrious pagan dead, his followers had chosen to become naturalized citizens of a republic that existed only in their minds, a republic of words, an empire of grammar. Ramus took a step in the direction of expatriation with his French *Dialectique*. He was no longer conversing with the ancients. He took from them what he needed. They had taught him to think, but he was ready to strip the ancient languages of their sacred aura. He was no longer addressing the dead. He was speaking to the living and his vision was fixed on a future when mankind, with the help of philosophy, would become better, more educated, more enlightened.[40]

At the beginning of his career, Ramus had been a militant of the humanist cause. His attempt to convert the university to his cause had failed. Outside of his own college, he had met only with hostility. The university as a whole chose to sink into oblivion rather than give up Aristotle. In defense of the University of Paris, however, it is worth pointing out that its allergic reaction to new ideas was characteristic of early modern universities.

Ramus found, at his own expense, that the university was an institution that no longer served the function it had in the past. Universities were medieval institutions. They could not leave behind their clerical complexion or embrace the kind of socratizing Ramus had in mind. His headlong rush toward pagan philosophy in its most daring aspects triggered the defense mechanisms of a medieval corporation dominated by the theology faculty.

In 1543, Ramus was merely censored for raising his voice against Aristotle, that is to say, against the doctors of theology. In 1624, long after Ramus had been murdered in his study, probably at the instigation of his conservative colleagues, the doctors of the theology faculty went beyond censorship: they requested and obtained a court order providing the death penalty for anyone foolhardy enough to criticize Aristotle.[41] In between these two historic episodes—Ramus's condemnation in 1543 and the court order of 1624—the process that Ramus had set in motion was completed. Those who wished to follow in Ramus's wake, those who chose "to travel the great highway of Reason,"[42] as his disciple Estienne Pasquier puts it, would have to make travel plans whose route circumvented the university, gave the university and everything it stood for a wide berth.

In this way a new type of intellectual was born. He was no longer a doctor of philosophy or even a master of arts. In the course of the two hundred years between the time Ramus was forbidden to teach philosophy and Voltaire achieved fame, there was hardly a significant scholar, scientist, or man of letters in France who was a master or a doctor of the university.

The new intellectual kept his distance from the university. He described himself as a *philosophe* and wrote in French—an easy, informal French for a nonacademic readership. This *philosophe* wore his learning lightly. He was perfectly at home with the ancients but quick to note that the ancient languages should be studied "not for their own sake, but simply as the means to an end."[43] He had little patience with those who studied Greek "only to discuss the meaning of a word." This kind of learning struck the *philosophe* formed in Ramus's school as pedantic, "*un sçavoir pedantesque.*"[44] He had tasks awaiting his attention more urgent than "enlightening posterity about the meter of Plautus's verse or the true spelling of a Latin word."[45] For that matter, he refused "to accord antiquity too much respect": this was for him "a form of superstition."[46] In a playful mood, he was prepared to challenge "all the propositions of those who in ancient times thought they were wise."[47] His task was to employ straight thinking in the service of humanity. He was not concerned with the classroom, the lecture hall, the Latin disputation. He was an adult, a citizen, "*un citoyen du monde, un homme d'estat,*"[48] ready to do battle against ignorance and superstition, which make men the slaves of custom.

4

Liberté, Egalité, Fraternité

SLAVES OF CUSTOM, men cannot imagine a better world. This is the chief complaint of the *philosophes*. In its most provocative and incisive form, it is expressed in a speech composed by a young law student, La Boétie, at some point between 1548 and 1553. It was not intended for publication. As is so often the case, even with rather prominent persons who die young and who shun publicity in the course of their brief lives, very little is known about the author of this passionate work variously known as *Contr'un* or *Discours de la Servitude Volontaire*.[1]

It was published, some years after the author's death, by French Protestants in exile who interpreted it as an attack on the arbitrary policies of the King of France. La Boétie did allude to contemporary events, at least in passing, if rather subtly, but the target he was aiming at was considerably broader than that presented by the personality or the policies of Henri II. The *Servitude* was a broadside fired against injustice and repression throughout history. The measures its author recommended for mankind's emancipation were meant to be applicable everywhere and at all times.

La Boétie was a young man when he wrote the *Servitude*, but he was no younger than a number of like-minded students who flirted with dangerous ideas. Montaigne, who was to become La Boétie's closest friend and lifelong admirer, and who played the part of Plato to La Boétie's Socrates, reports that he read the *Servitude* in manuscript before he ever set eyes on its author, whom he was predisposed to admire when he met him at last. Montaigne was only 20 when the 23-year-old La Boétie arrived in Bordeaux, fresh from Law School and already appointed to a judgeship.[2]

In later years, Montaigne prudently attempted to lower his late friend's profile as a radical philosopher by claiming that the notorious *Servitude* was no more than a youthful indiscretion composed at the age of 18 or even 16, but the fact remains that Montaigne admired the work at 20, continued to admire it as long as he lived, and judged it to be the chief claim to posterity's admiration of a man who had no equal. Montaigne never met "anyone who could be compared to him" and he had "no doubt at all that he believed what he wrote, for he was so conscientious that he would not lie even in jest." Another thing Montaigne knew about his friend is that "he would rather have been born in Venice than in Sarlat, and with reason," meaning that he would have preferred to live as the citizen of a republic rather than as the subject of a king.[3]

Not that La Boëtie fared poorly as a French subject. He was born with a silver spoon in his mouth, in a splendid mansion which may still be admired today, right in the heart of the town of Sarlat, in the Perigord region, not very far from Montaigne's family property. As the son of an important royal official and the nephew of a Chief Justice of the Bordeaux Appeals Court, his career trajectory was determined at birth. Where he studied before he registered as a student at the Law School of the University of Orléans is anyone's guess. The Bordeaux college would have been a reasonable option, although he could have studied at Agen too, without being too far from home. There is no evidence that he attended any of these schools. This does not mean much. Unlike Montaigne or Pasquier, La Boëtie did not seem interested in reminiscing about his school days, either because he never reached the age when one reminisces, or because he was educated at home, in the latter case surely by tutors of very high caliber.

It does seem likely that he spent some time in Paris before going on to Orléans, but, there again, there is no solid evidence. All that can be said for certain is that his law degree was issued at Orléans in September of 1553 and that he was a protégé of Michel de l'Hospital, a truly rare figure who owed his appointment as Chancellor of the Kingdom neither to high birth nor to great wealth but strictly to his merit.[4]

L'Hospital was very much the intellectuals' politician, an erudite and liberal man, who wrote Latin poetry and went out of his way to hold off the fanatical impulses triggered by religious conflict. It was L'Hospital who introduced Ronsard at Court, in December of 1552, bringing him to the attention of the King, the Queen and the Cardinal de Lorraine. As an adroit impresario of literary careers, L'Hospital advised Ronsard to dedicate some poems to the eminent bishop of Riez, Lancelot de Carle, who was a scholar, a Hellenist and a man of letters. La Boëtie married the bishop's sister, Marguerite, about that time. It seems likely that his connection with the Ronsard group, if it was not already established, was in place by 1554, at the latest.[5]

By that time, the *Discours de la Servitude Volontaire* was circulating in manuscript. The *Servitude*, which runs to 57 pages in Paul Bonnefon's edition, contains nothing that would have occasioned much surprise among the *habitués* of Brinon's circle or in the classrooms of Ramus' college, nothing that an eminent patron like L'Hospital or a graduate of the Bordeaux college like Montaigne would have disagreed with.

Fed by the same sources that supplied the raw material of the Parisian *philosophes'* conversations—Cicero, Plato, Horace, Lucretius, among others—the *Servitude* was written in French and destined to be talked about and passed along as a clandestine manuscript too dangerous to be printed but admired by intellectuals who were adept at extrapolating radical imperatives from two-thousand-year-old philosophical writings. The Italian scholar J. Corbinelli, who served as tutor to the young prince who would reign, eventually, as King Henri III, saw a manuscript copy of the *Servitude* and described it to a correspondent as "an erudite and profound, but dangerous, work." In the same spirit, the French writer Scévole de Sainte Marthe thought that La Boëtie touched upon "delicate and disturbing" problems, but that the *Servitude* was "conceived with somewhat more freedom than the times were prepared to accept."[6]

As a private statement, not destined for publication, La Boëtie's polemic against tyranny spells out the political implications of an education in the Parisian style more fully and in a less cautious way than any other document I know of. The *Servitude* also allows us to measure the distance which separates the "contemplative" philosophers of ancient Athens, as understood by their Roman disciples, from the state of mind of Renaissance Frenchmen familiar with the ancient arguments. There is an urgency about La Boëtie's writing, a passion, an earnestness that captures the reader's attention. This is no desultory set piece in imitation of Cicero. It is a call to action, even though the axioms on which the argument rests are grounded in Graeco-Roman sources.

What stands out in this work is its uncompromising tone. A prudent *philosophe* like Montaigne may well agree, thirty years later and anonymously, that democracy and constitutional government are to be preferred to monarchy, but La Boëtie treats monarchy as an unnatural vice whose consequences are deadly and which must be rooted out. The author shows his impatience with academic political theory from the start by refusing to engage in the usual discussion of the various forms of government and fuss about with the question of which is to be preferred. As far as he is concerned, monarchy is not a legitimate form of government at all, but an outlaw aberration, since there can be nothing legitimate about one man's rule over millions of his brothers.[7]

Brothers? Yes. For La Boëtie, and, indeed, for all the *philosophes* we have encountered so far, if there is anything at all that is "clear and apparent in Nature"—so clear, indeed, "that it is impermissible to be blind to it"—it is that Nature "has made us all in the same shape and, it would seen, formed in the same mold, so that we may know each other as companions or, rather, as brothers."[8] This unshakable conviction surely has its origin in the classroom, but what is mentioned only in passing, or merely implied, by the *optimi auctores*, becomes, in La Boétie's reading, the cornerstone of his philosophy.

We are all equal by nature. Some of us may be naturally smarter or stronger than others, but such differences are not to be misinterpreted as Nature's invitation for the strong to exploit the weak. Nature did not intend to set down the weaker ones among us in this world as prey exposed to the attacks of the stronger. On the contrary, affirms La Boétie, Nature's "intention was to give the more capable among us a chance to exercise brotherly affection (*fraternelle affection*)."[9]

If the original and natural brotherhood of human beings is the most certain of axioms, it is also beyond doubt for La Boétie that we all come into this world endowed with certain rights and certain natural inclinations. Instinctive in nature, these inclinations force us to obey our parents, to subject our minds to Reason, and to acknowledge no masters. Nature has given us the ability to speak, so as to encourage the "mutual declaration of our thoughts" and the "communion of our individual wills." Nature, in short, meant us to be united, "to be as one." It is not possible to doubt that by nature we were all meant to be free.[10]

How did it come about, then, that most of mankind does in fact live in conditions of abject servitude? Are Princes in possession of some secret and devastating weapon which enables them to turn their brothers into slaves? When La Boétie speaks of Princes, he makes no distinction between hereditary monarchs and those who are elected to their office. Neither of these rules legitimately. With the exception of direct democracy, no form of government meets La Boétie's test of legitimacy. How does it happen that one man can force a million of his brothers to serve him miserably, their necks held down under yokes, like oxen? "Oh God, what is this? What shall we call it? What vice is this? To see an infinite number of persons obey—no, serve; to see them governed—no, tyrannized; having nothing they can call their own, neither goods nor relatives, neither wives nor children, not even their own lives!"[11] And who is it who forces them to give up their freedom? Is it a terrifying army against which they are defenseless? Nothing of the sort. Men choose freely to serve their execrable masters. Had they the slightest wish to regain their natural freedom, they could easily do it. There would be no need to take up arms, to conspire, to revolt, to risk anything at all. Nothing would be easier than to put an end to this subjection which is voluntarily incurred. A tyrant's power depends on one thing alone: the acquiescence of his subjects.[12]

"Poor, miserable, senseless peoples," thunders the youthful moralist, "you allow him to take away your wealth, to pillage your fields, steal your houses, remove your ancient family possessions." Worse, "you raise your daughters so that he may have his pleasure with them, you raise your sons so that he may lead them to his wars, to be butchered." And why are you so fearful of this tyrant? "Your master has only two eyes, two hands, one body. He is in no way different from the least among you." You fear him? "Resolve to serve him no longer—and you are free! (*vous voilà libres*)."[13]

Liberté, we are reminded, is "so great and pleasant a possession" that, once it is lost, all evils follow, one after the other. Since it would be so easy to regain their freedom, the question that needs to be pursued is why men have almost universally lost their desire to be free. "Let us research this problem (*cherchons donc par conjecture*)," the author advises, as though he fears that the question has become academic. Likening the abject servility of men to a disease which gives every sign of being incurable, he admits that there is little hope of cutting out the cancerous growth that is "the stubborn will to serve." Even the desire for liberty no longer seems natural to men. By what means has man lost his original nature, he who, alone, was born to live freely? How has he lost the very memory of his original nature and the desire to regain it?[14]

The answer proposed is that it is custom which is to blame. Suppose, La Boëtie suggests, as a thought-experiment, "suppose that some new race of men were to come into this world now, accustomed neither to subjection nor to freedom, knowing nothing about either condition, not even understanding the meaning of the words." Suppose you gave these brand-new people a choice between slavery and freedom. Wouldn't they, as a matter of course, prefer to live freely, according to laws they themselves would devise? Wouldn't they choose to obey Reason alone, rather than subject themselves to the arbitrary power of one man?[15]

Unlike these hypothetical beings, most of us have fallen victim, long ago, to the powerful force of custom.[16] In his attempt to explain this catastrophic truth, La Boëtie supposes that it is an unequal struggle that opposes the natural love of liberty in us to the seductions engineered by custom. In the contest between nature and nurture, the latter, he assumes, is, by far, the most powerful protagonist. The "seeds of goodness" which Nature has planted in us must be so fragile, he suspects, that they cannot resist the slightest pressure.[17] Hence, when tyrants set about enslaving their brothers, they encounter little resistance. In time, the very memory of freedom vanishes. Remind these abject slaves of the attractions of liberty, try to rouse them from their torpor, tell them they need not allow themselves to be harnessed like oxen—and what will they reply? They will say that they have always been subjects, that their fathers were subjects before them, that they have no choice but to endure their bitter fate.[18]

Their resignation, one might argue, is, in part, at least, the result of the clever strategies of those who exploit them. Tyrants are shrewd, they know how to "dumb down" (*abestir*) their subjects, they know how to distract them by catering to their vilest instincts. When the Persian monarch Cyrus faced a revolt, he set up brothels, taverns, and public games. He never had any trouble after that, so gullible are men. Theaters, games, spectacles, gladiators, circuses—those were the instruments of tyranny in ancient times.[19] The tyrant's goal is to drug his subjects into stupor (*drogueries*). In this way, the masses, robbed of their critical faculties (*assotis*), pleased by all these amusements, soon became used to following orders as innocently as children.[20]

When circuses do not suffice to keep the masses in line, there is always religion. Most of the ancient monarchs pretended that they were more than human and that they could perform miracles. Tyrants like to use religion as a shield and hide behind the appearance of divinity so that they may continue to lead deplorable lives.[21]

While entertainments and miracles are certainly effective tools for controlling the masses, nothing is more important, from the tyrants' point of view, than thought control, and nothing more dangerous than the presence of educated persons. The Turkish Sultan understands this very well. He makes sure that there are no men of learning in his empire. Books and learning, more than anything else, prepare us to understand and to hate tyranny.[22] This is where there is room for hope, since, even under the worst sort of tyranny, even in a world in which books are censored and in which the mass of the population has lost sight of the very meaning of liberty, there will always be a few of us who feel the weight of the yoke and who wish to shake it off. Such men will never get used to being slaves, they will never be able to forget the privileges Nature endowed them with at birth. Because of their natural intelligence and imagination, they will not be content, like the mass of the population, with looking no further than what lies in front of their feet. They understand the past, they think about the future, they are able to judge the present. Such men will never get used to having masters. Even if liberty were to be lost entirely, and nowhere to be found on earth, they would be able to imagine it in their minds, to feel it and to savor it.[23]

As for those ordinary mortals who make up the overwhelming majority, they are trapped in a web from which it is difficult to escape. The secret of domination is not, in La Boëtie's estimation, brute force and terror, "not troops of cavalry, not companies of infantry, not palace guards and secret police." The truth is that tyrants rule with the assistance of four or five men who dominate their country. It has always been this way. Five or six are the tyrant's accomplices. Those six can count on the support of six hundred who profit under their patronage. The six hundred, in turn, divide up their spoils with six thousand others, to whom they allot the governing of counties and the collection of taxes. After that comes the crowd which follows in the wake of the six thousand, so that, in the end, they are not six thousand, but a hundred thousand, they are millions linked, as if by a single rope, to the tyrant at the top. In sum, tyrants, devourers of people (*mange-peuples*) use some of their subjects to control the rest.[24]

This is a clear-eyed description of power relations in France. Its most dangerous component is La Boëtie's visceral hatred of monarchs. This would have been the main reason for circulating the manuscript clandestinely, among like-minded readers who would appreciate it without being scandalized by it. The author's expressed preference for direct democracy could have been made palatable if only he had not chosen to speak in his own voice. The same radical critique of the established order of things, of civilization in its current form, could be expressed openly by choosing a suitable stratagem to disguise the author's conviction. Without having to resort to descriptions of fictitious utopian communities, as Thomas More had done, or to fictitious conversations with Native Americans, as Montaigne would do, one could for instance, write approvingly about democracy in seemingly objective commentaries devoted to historical events in the distant past. Hardly anyone was bothered by the praise commonly lavished upon ancient Greek democracy. La Boëtie was certainly not alone in praising Greek liberty in the manner of Herodotus. Where Roman history was concerned, it was by no means unusual to look back to republican virtues, as Cicero and Tacitus had done.

In just such a way, Professor Ramus, without standing accused of being a revolutionary, was able to write about the ancient Gauls whom Caesar conquered, and to depict these ancestors of the French as a nation in love with liberty, equality and fraternity. Like much of Ramus' work, the *Traicté des façons et coustumes des anciens Gaulois* is remarkable for its originality.[25] To write a book about the customs and the way of life of a people without history is a remarkable idea. As in the case of Pierre Belon's *Observations*, the author was doing something so new that there was no recognized category into which his book could be fitted.

It was not an *histoire*, in the usual sense. Unlike Caesar, Ramus was not giving an account of a military campaign. He was interested in the "*histoire morale*"[26] of his ancestors, that is to say, in an account of their *moeurs* or *mores*. The second edition of Castelnau's translation would, in fact, carry the title of *Traitté des meurs des anciens gaulois*. The history of *moeurs*, the history of the value-system of an ancient people, this was a new kind of project which was to have a long and successful career.

For what was it, after all, that a *philosophe* was interested in when he studied the past? Not the ephemeral idiot's tale of battles and portents, but the way in which people led their lives, more or less virtuously. There were useful lessons to be learned from such investigations, since all men, everywhere and at all times are bound to be alike in their essence, if not in the particulars of their daily lives. It was, unfortunately, impossible to observe the ancient Gauls as closely and as reliably as Belon observed the Turks and as others observed the native tribes of the New World.

A philosophically minded researcher writing in Paris in the 1550s had very little to go on in his search for well-documented accounts of the primitive Celtic tribes that roamed the Seine valley two thousand years earlier. Even an intelligent contemporary like Julius Caesar could not be trusted when he reported on the illiterate forest dwellers on the outer frontiers of the Roman world. He was hardly an impartial reporter. The Gauls were his enemies. It was not part of his purpose to find good things to say about them, nor was he very interested in studying the culture of the people he subdued. He was concerned, above all, with the military aspects of his experiences, with the shaping of his own reputation and with practical lessons for future colonial ventures.

Ramus was interested in something else. He hoped to discover a few reasonably credible facts about the social organization and the culture of the Gauls. Certainty, in such matters, was beyond anyone's reach, he believed. The data were not available for an "*histoire certaine*" (*la recherche seroit bien grande et malaisée*), in view of the fact that the Gauls left no written records.[27] One could not expect to reconstruct past events in the absence of credible contemporary sources. So it is only a rough idea of what the Gauls were like that one could hope for, at best.

Caesar's account of his wars against the Gauls is surely the best source for "our history." In spite of his biases and limitations, Caesar understood, at least approximately, what the Gauls were about. The modern *philosophe* has to be a discriminating observer, looking over Caesar's shoulder, challenging his conclusions when necessary, discarding much of what the Roman general considers worth reporting as irrelevant to the *histoire morale* of the Gauls. Where Caesar's account is most frustratingly inadequate, one can try turning to other, less direct, sources, such as Tacitus' report on the Germanic tribes to the north, for instance. There was, after all, Ramus believes, some considerable similarity—even "*fraternité*"—in the way German, Belgian, Parisian or British tribes behaved. Where Caesar fails to inform the reader about matters of consequence, such as the weaponry of the Celtic tribes, Ramus will supplement his main source by turning to other credible reports.[28]

Caesar surely followed his own agenda, but Ramus has an agenda of his own. In his less guarded moments, he paints a romantic and admiring picture of those whom he considers his ancestors. He is quick to defend the Gauls against accusations of drunkenness and lascivious inclinations, of primitive manners or "façons barbares."[29] When he is not defending the honor of the Gauls, he deploys a general theory of civilization which is not without classical antecedents, but is, nevertheless, modern in every sense. He assumes—and, soon, other amateur anthropologists such as Montaigne and La Popelinière,[30] writing about American natives, will concur—that civilization is a natural process at work everywhere in much the same way. When Caesar reports that the Gauls, and other tribes he encounters, all seem very serious about honoring visitors, treating strangers "as if they were sacred," plying them with gifts, presenting them with the best cuts of meat at their banquets,[31] Ramus is quick to note the similarities between the practices of Celtic and Germanic tribal leaders and those of "the Greek chieftains of whom Homer writes."[32]

There appears to be some natural form of generosity which is exhibited by tribal societies before they come into contact with a more "civilized" way of life. The "brusque simplicity" of the Germanic tribesmen is compared, in Ramus' reflections, with the elaborate and less virile habits of the urban Greeks and Romans, in the wake of Tacitus.[33] This comparison then serves as the starting point of a theory of historical development. Caesar's album of primitive tribesmen is interesting, certainly. What modern Frenchman could resist these unique impressions of their ancestors' appearance? They were savages, one has to grant, who painted their naked bodies, wore elaborate and menacing hairdos, lurched into battle screaming imprecations and boasting of their prowess. They built no cities, bridges or ships, they lived in simple thatched huts, ate their meals sitting on the ground, and took, far too easily, to the trashier blandishments of their civilized neighbors, especially where the consumption of alcoholic beverages was concerned.[34]

All this may be true, but the Roman general's impressions, which suggest that he was facing a childlike race of bullies and cowards, are superficial impressions only. They do not allow the reader to grasp the inner life of these volatile creatures whose world was being obliterated by colonial conquest. What was their language? Did they have a way of recording their deeds? Was theirs a purely oral culture, entrusted to the care of their Druids, who were natural poets in the manner of Homer? Unfortunately, we will never know, so ruthlessly was their culture destroyed. "What a shame," comments Ramus, in one of his fervently patriotic moments, "what a shame that Frenchmen must study long and hard to learn Greek and Latin, so that they may read Homer, Demosthenes, Virgil or Cicero, when they could, instead, be singing the hymns and poems of their own national bards effortlessly and with pleasure," in their own language.[35]

This sentimental affinity with blue-painted warriors assembled in forest clearings is one aspect of Ramus' interpretation of the past. It soon becomes clear that he has something else on his mind, as he reads Caesar's memoirs. What Ramus sets out to discover, reading between the lines of Caesar's sober text, is a utopian vision of a virtuous society that both ancient Romans and modern Frenchmen must admire. Caesar may have seen only fur-clad savages, but Ramus sees something else, prompted by Caesar's own observations.[36] These people were primitive indeed, so primitive, notes Ramus, that "they did not even know which land belonged to whom."[37] They had not as yet discovered the concept of private property. The Gauls, like their Germanic relatives, were communists. They held land in common (*Ils n'ont point de terre qui soit particuliere*). This "*égalité*" was the key to their happiness. Private property, in Ramus' view, is the source of all evils. Agreeing with Plato, Ramus considers wealth and poverty "the two chief plagues of mankind." The communism of the Germanic tribes is to be valued more highly than Plato's theories, since Plato "only imagined the idea of a happy Republic," while the northern barbarians "actually achieved it," by means of their "good customs."[38]

Such customs may have struck Aristotle or Caesar as "barbaric,"[39] but on closer examination, even the effeminate Greeks (*ces petits delicats de Grecs*) could only look with admiration at the effectiveness of the spartan régime followed by the forest tribes. No cities, no money, no private property, not even farming, at times. Theirs was a semi-nomadic existence. They were herders of cattle, hunters and warriors. Their simple life was the source of their virtues and the foundation of their "*tres heureuse republique*."[40]

They went about naked, covered only in part with the pelts of animals. They ate out of crude pottery, sitting on dog pelts. They bathed at dawn, before breakfast. They may not have been "*civilisez*," but they were happy. Contact with Roman civilization served only to corrupt these naturally virtuous people, as Caesar himself appears to acknowledge in his comments on the tribes which lived beyond the reach of Roman wine merchants.[41]

Before they abandoned their original simplicity and traded *barbarie* for *civilité*,[42] the Germans were noted for their humanity and liberty.[43] They scorned gold, they were chaste and honorable. Theirs was a society of frugal equals, whose liberty may be compared to that enjoyed by Roman citizens before their republic was transformed into a rapacious empire.[44] The Gauls, unlike the Romans, knew how to prevent the rise of tyrants. It was their

Constitution, "*le gouvernement des Republiques Gauloises,*"[45] which provided the safeguards needed to preserve liberty. Their "*Republique Democratique*" was so constituted that war leaders were chosen by popular acclamation. These chieftains, once invested with their commands, were never in a position to oppress their people. Had they tried to overstep their authority, their mandate would have lapsed.[46]

Professor Ramus' treatise on the customs of the ancient Gauls was not a *rêverie* or a secular sermon. It was a scholarly investigation founded on trustworthy reports. It is true that the author's patriotic fervor leads him astray, on occasion. His intention was to use historical sources which would allow him to reach incontrovertible conclusions. Following in the wake of philologists such as Beatus Rhenanus, Ramus was prepared to argue with his sources and to set legends aside in order to prove that historical research, which may not achieve certainty in most instances, can, at least, clear the ground, dispel falsehoods, and provide a modest beginning for understanding the world as it really is. Understanding, for instance, that the so-called Franks, thought of as the ancestors of the French nobility, were not Trojan heroes of exalted Homeric ancestry, but Germanic war bands. Ramus knew the work of Beatus Rheanus who demonstrated this in 1531, but he avoids a frontal assault on the Trojan legend. He was, after all, writing about a historical period which preceded the arrival of the Franks. At some time in the future, he explains, he may turn to this topic, to the whole question of the Frankish conquest of Gaul. As it happens, it was his student, Estienne Pasquier, who took up the challenge, a few months after the publication of Ramus' treatise, no doubt at Ramus' suggestion.

5

Historical Research in the
Service of Philosophy

P<small>ASQUIER GRADUATED FROM</small> Ramus' school in 1546, at the age of 17. At 20, he was practicing law. He remained close to Ramus for many years. In 1559, when Ramus was publishing his treatise on the ancient Gauls, Pasquier still lived next door to his old college, subletting a portion of Omer Talon's apartment.[1] Although he had already, by then, established his reputation as a writer, publishing a playful dialogue of the sort that was appreciated in Brinon's circle under the title *Le Monophile* (1554),[2] his chief interest was in historical scholarship.

He made his first excursion into this field in the wake of Ramus' *Gauls*, publishing the first book of his *Recherches de la France* in 1560.[3] In the opening chapters of this book, he covered the same ground Ramus had just surveyed, offering his readers a series of commentaries and reflections on Caesar's account of his wars in Gaul, and defending the national honor against charges of barbarism. Unlike his mentor, Pasquier did not look for traces of an "*heureuse republique*" in Caesar's comments on Celtic customs. Less of a theorist than Ramus, Pasquier was concerned, above all, with the difficulty of writing a truthful account of events in the distant past on the basis of fragmentary sources, but he did not hide his philosophy, which was in tune with the democratic ideals expressed by Ramus and La Boëtie.

Addressing the reader, Pasquier wrote: "I have made up my mind that I will dedicate this book without flattery, to you alone, whatever your social standing may be." Instead of dedicating his book to the Cardinal of Lorraine or to some other powerful patron who could be expected to shower favors upon him, Pasquier chose to stand apart and to make a show of independence. "Why should I flatter myself and make myself believe, falsely, that some great lord is listening to me and is favorably inclined toward me, and why should I pretend to offer this book to such a lord, writing a grandiloquent and hypocritical dedication to him, when I know that he will not even trouble to read its title page? So it is to you, reader, that I present this book."[4]

I do not doubt that there might have been some among Pasquier's colleagues and acquaintances who took offense, thinking that it was easy for Pasquier, who was independently wealthy—sufficiently so, in any case, to require no subsidies—to grandstand in this way, displaying his contempt for impoverished academics who were obliged to write flattering dedications to their patrons. This was not an affectation, however, on Pasquier's part. He was consistent in his criticism of such practices, which he thought of as demeaning. In a letter to Ronsard, four years before the publication of his *Recherches*, Pasquier had already taken it upon himself to criticize the poet for his "*servitude à demy courtisane*," his courtier's tendency, that is, to flatter great lords in his verses. Ronsard's name-dropping set Pasquier's teeth on edge. In a mixture of exquisite courtesy and firm principle, he tells Ronsard that he is, of course, "pleased to be mentioned in the poet's verses, for he will never be sorry that posterity will know that Ronsard and Pasquier, in their lifetime, were friends," but, even as he thanks the poet, he advises him to "stop using his pen so cheaply" and condemns his practice of praising those whom "both of us know to be without merit."[5]

Pasquier was very much aware of the novelty of his *Recherches*. He described Ramus, Copernicus, and Paracelsus as the "three great heretics or innovators of our time."[6] Modesty prevented him from adding his own name to this constellation, as the fourth star and as the creator of a revolutionary approach to the past, as new and full of consequences, in its way, as was Copernicus' rethinking of celestial mechanics.

He was not prepared to say so in 1560, but in later editions of the *Recherches* he would state clearly just what he believed was new about his researches and why, for that matter, he had to invent a new name for what he was doing, since he was not writing a history in the sense in which others before him had composed histories. The ancients had written contemporary history, eyewitness history, recording events that occurred in their own lifetime, as in the case of Caesar. Or else they wrote compilations, stringing together and paraphrasing older accounts. Pasquier's contemporaries considered historical writing literature, composing dramatic stories, inventing dialogue for their protagonists, and paying lip service only to the notion that history should be a true account of what happened. "The passage of time has a way of investing one's writings with authority," ran their argument, according to Pasquier. Their books, they claimed, "may not seem entirely plausible to begin with," but, eventually, "they will appear trustworthy and will acquire their own indisputable authority, as indeed, has happened in the case of the ancients."[7]

Pasquier evidently had no intention of relying on the passage of time to endow his work with authority. Instead, he set out to apply to the medieval history of France the methods developed by philologists and jurists, methods which relied on an exhaustive examination of all available original sources, however fragmentary and obscure, to reconstruct and interpret ancient texts. Given the paucity of reliable sources for the history of medieval France, especially for the early centuries, Pasquier found it impossible to put together a coherent account of events. He opted instead for a series of investigations, some of them inconclusive, which he decided to call *Recherches*.

His first move was to brush aside all existing accounts which claimed to be histories of France. None of them, in his estimation, were founded on facts. The past, in his view, was a vast *terra incognita* covered with seemingly impenetrable growths which would have to be cleared away and replaced by "*conjectures*" founded on original sources alone. He was determined "to say nothing of importance without proof."[8] Not that he expected his *conjectures* to lead to unassailable truths every time, but let those who would come after him "and who sail in the same waters" correct him. This should be easy enough, since he had already shown the way and "broken the ice," he adds, comparing his innovations to the discoveries made by intrepid explorers in arctic waters.[9]

Pasquier made a practice of citing his sources scrupulously. It was not his intention to make claims about the past which could not be backed with "ocular examples."[10] His method resembles that of Belon. He insists that his readers witness the proofs of his assertions with their own eyes. He expects them to touch the past with their fingers (*toucher au doigt*).[11] He may have been talking with Pierre Belon and reading his *Observations*, which had just been published, when he entered the debate concerning the part that climate plays in determining the rise and fall of civilizations.

In a letter of 1554, he rejects climate as a factor in the shaping of human history, on the evidence of the "ocular example" of Greece. Was there ever a greater assemblage of first-rate minds in one place than in Greece, two thousand years ago? The climate surely has not changed dramatically since, yet what is there to be found in Greece now, other than "*barbarie*"?[12] Such reflections served to enliven the learned discussions (*rencontres*) Pasquier was in the habit of participating in.[13] To make more than a general debating point, however, one needed proof of a sort that no one could argue with.

That was the kind of proof he was prepared to provide when he took on the controversial topic of French origins. Who were the Franks, that mysterious people who invaded Gaul, defeating Celts and Romans to become the founders of the French monarchy? The fashionable story, repeated in official chronicles, was that the Franks were really Trojans. Somehow, having been driven out of Troy by the wrath of Achilles, they had wandered along the Danube Valley for thousands of years before they reached their promised land, France, at last.[14]

This cherished myth, the staple of official propaganda, gave Pasquier a fine opportunity to show what a philosophical historian could do. The object of the exercise was to strip the past of lies, especially of the fatuously embellished confections produced by hacks in the service of the Court. By choosing to attack the myth of Trojan origins, Pasquier was sure to attract attention. This was a hallowed legend no French writer had, so far, been prepared to repudiate. It was a legitimizing myth, of a piece with the miraculous events said to have attended the baptism of Clovis, the first Frankish king to accept Christianity, according to the chroniclers. La Boëtie had already made the point, in private, that monarchs and their accomplices invented such stories to legitimize their usurpation of power.[15] Unlike La Boëtie, Pasquier does not adopt the stance of a moralist. He does not denounce conspirators. His approach is not adversarial. In the long "war against ignorance," which would continue into the eighteenth century, Pasquier was among the earliest successful combatants. He created an arsenal of ideological weapons whose power proceeded from historical scholarship—from those "ocular demonstrations" which appeared irrefutable.

In the case of the origin of the Franks, the detective work had already been done some years earlier by the German philologist Beatus Rhenanus, who had demonstrated that the Franks were Germanic warrior bands.[16] Beatus' demonstration, published in Latin and rather technical in nature, was meant for an audience of specialists. Pasquier set about making Beatus' results palatable to a broad, non-academic public.

To demolish the legend of the exalted Trojan ancestry of the French nation was to enter a forbidden zone as surely as Ramus had done when he issued a wholesale challenge to the authority of Aristotle. The terrain in which Ramus chose to do battle was of a different sort, however. His dispute had been with the University. He had conducted it in Latin and according to the savage customs of medieval universities, which required debaters to heap scorn on their opponents in grossly exaggerated ways.

Pasquier wrote with a different audience in mind. For this audience, he devised techniques of persuasion which were to be adopted by later generations of *philosophes*. Writing in an easy, informal French, he taught his readers to scorn lies and poor thinking. He taught them, at the same time, to avoid the pedantry of academics. Where Ramus fought Ignorance with the equivalent of a battering ram, choosing frontal assault as his preferred modus operandi, Pasquier placed depth charges, with great delicacy, at the foot of seemingly indestructible beliefs sacred to traditionalists. Although his purpose was entirely serious, he became a master of the art of persiflage, mocking with great courtesy, as Tahureau recommended, and thus inaugurating a formula for *déniaisement* of lasting effectiveness.

Distancing himself from his academic colleagues even while he was turning to an arcane and difficult field of inquiry, Pasquier defended himself against the charge of being an "*antiquaire*"—someone who collected and deciphered old manuscripts solely for the pleasure of it. It was a temptation, he admitted, a temptation the philosophical historian should avoid at all costs, "as navigators avoid reefs at sea."[17] Although he chose the earliest history of the French as his testing ground, he was not doing this in the spirit of an antiquarian. His purpose was to show that self-serving fictions were not useful to the public and that it was possible to achieve, instead, at least a modest understanding of what really happened by distinguishing between authentic contemporary sources and later accounts. This basic distinction, which is the foundation on which the modern historical method was built, was not as yet generally accepted in Pasquier's lifetime.

In his investigation of French beginnings Pasquier adopted a properly critical approach. "It appears that none of our historians have a clue when it comes to this question."[18] There is a good reason for this, he believes. The ancient Greek and Roman authors, whose reports were the only contemporary sources which could conceivably contain information about the fierce, illiterate tribes to the north, simply knew very little about them. The Greeks, it seems, got it all wrong (*en parlerent à la traverse*).[19] The Romans, who were constantly at war with the Germanic tribes, and ought to have been better informed, nevertheless failed to provide a clear picture, at least in those of their books which happened to survive. One thing, at least, can be established firmly by studying the sketchy observations to be found in the writings of Caesar, Tacitus, Pliny, Ptolemy, Strabo, Ammianus Marcellinus, and the Scriptores Historiae Augustae: the earlier writers had never heard of the Franks.[20]

At some point in the fourth century, the Franks seem to step out of their anonymity, all of a sudden. Given this long and mysterious lacuna in their history, it is no wonder that enterprising and imaginative modern writers feel free to spin tales about the Franks. The common opinion, Pasquier reminds his readers, is that the Franks were heroic and noble refugees from the Trojan Wars who wandered along the Danube valley for centuries before they found their historical rôle at last and entered Gaul.

Now, says Pasquier, let us ask: where is the ancient author who tells us that the Franks are Trojans? Since there is no such source, let us drop this laboriously devised story which no respectable author will vouch for. If the Franks were not Trojans, who were they? Following Beatus' linguistic researches, Pasquier explains that they must have been Germanic tribes settled in the Rhine Delta. They entered Roman Gaul as the empire weakened. Among the causes of the empire's weakness was the adoption of Christianity by

Constantine, whose conversion was not brought about, in Pasquier's opinion, by miracles, or by the emperor's religious conviction, but by political considerations, namely Constantine's strategy of attracting Christians to his party in the course of his deadly rivalry with Licinius.[21]

Pasquier treats the French claim to Trojan ancestry as a pardonable form of vanity, something very much like the vanity of families looking for noble ancestry. Historians ready to please their readers will claim Trojan ancestry for many nations, linking their fate to that old story of the Trojan Wars which "Greek fables mention." As for himself, Pasquier adds wryly, he cannot see why one would wish to be descended from the Trojans who were, after all, a defeated nation, if the story is true. What if it isn't true? Suppose Troy was never captured, suppose the Trojan survivors never set out to wander westward, then where shall we say the French come from? Let us forget all these far-fetched tales, he concludes, which are based only on stories told by monks, and face the fact that the Franks were Germanic tribes which set out from the Rhine delta.[22] Pasquier's first demonstration of the uses historical criticism could be put to was followed by many others, most of them calculated attacks on false notions and most of them intended to expose the naïveté of medieval chroniclers and other unphilosophical amateurs. Controversial in nature, many of Pasquier's *recherches* circulated only in manuscript for years, especially in those bitter years when religious zealots intimidated those who showed no sign of joining one party or another.

Although Pasquier went out of his way to avoid modern history, which was too dangerous a territory for an impartial historian to venture into,[23] he could not avoid giving offense—even when he wrote about events a thousand years in the past. Even posthumously, Pasquier kept on provoking violent reactions in those who feared the consequences of historical criticism.

The publication, in 1621, six years after the author's death, of the most complete edition of his *Recherches de la France*, caused a popular Jesuit preacher, François Garasse, to publish a 985-page review of the book in which he assaulted the late author in the name of all the worthy personages whom Pasquier had criticized, beginning with King Clovis.[24]

Garasse took the position that kings, popes, and emperors were above criticism. It was improper, to say the least, for a subject to express reservations about his superiors, argued Garasse. The contrast with Pasquier's outlook could not be sharper. "I will always belong to the party of those who follow the great path of Reason and refuse to deviate from it just to please the crowd," wrote Pasquier, in a letter to Ronsard, in 1555.[25] In the name of liberty, he was impatient with any and all signs of submission expressed by one person toward another. To address a man as "lord" struck Pasquier as a shameful departure from Nature's intention. "When they were free men, the Romans never employed the word *dominus*, which is the equivalent of our *sire* or *seigneur*," Pasquier points out. It was only when tyranny was established in Rome that flattery of this kind came into common usage, since "language tends to express our customs." This is why exaggerated expressions of submission and flattery are not surprising in the mouths of courtiers, whose use of words is filled with artifice: "The courtier, accustomed to wealth and grandeur, living a life of ease, has corrupted the purity of our language and created an effeminate grammar." To hear French spoken in its natural form, one has to listen to the speech of ordinary people.[26]

This respect for the qualities of the common people is present throughout Pasquier's reflections. In his desire to do away with artifice in any form, he was even ready to take on Professor Ramus. *"Or sus, je vous veux denoncer une forte guerre!"* he challenged his old friend and teacher playfully, when Ramus invented a new phonetic system to simplify French spelling conventions. The objective may be laudable, thought Pasquier, but the remedy Ramus proposed was too artificial. "Our ancestors," wrote Pasquier, "did not choose to spell in a particular way on a whim." Old customs, including the customary ways of spelling, should be allowed to develop naturally.[27]

Pasquier's respect for the common people may appear to be at odds with his denunciations of the *sotte multitude*, of that "many-headed beast" so easily led by the nose. Pasquier cites his favorite poet, Horace, both to justify his confidence in the common people's use of language and to express his fear of the mob's impulsive rages.[28] Torn between his genuine sympathy for *le peuple* and his well-founded fear of the excesses of which the masses were capable when misled by venal agitators, Pasquier on balance absolves the simple folk of responsibility. Writing to one of his sons, who was commanding a company of infantry in 1586, Pasquier pleads with him to spare the civilian population along his route. *"Ce pauvre peuple"* bears no responsibility for the murderous conflict of the civil wars, he explains. "They must be spared." He reminds his son, the captain, that he, too, is of the people.[29]

As a *philosophe*, Pasquier believes in the natural equality of human beings. Alas, it was an observable fact that the mass of the population could be moved to perform vicious and barbaric acts. Such behavior, however, was not natural: it was induced by demagogues, who exploited the common people's lack of sophistication. Their natural virtues had been replaced long ago by greed. It was the irresistible appeal of "those powerful words: Mine and Thine (*Mien et Tien*) which was the cause of all disturbances among most nations."[30] Short of returning mankind to its natural state, which did not seem feasible, the only way to restore virtue is to teach even the simplest peasants how to think effectively, so as to protect them from the designs of demagogues.[31]

Pasquier was just as convinced as Ramus had been that all human beings, regardless of their social background, were capable of reasoning and could be turned into *philosophes*.[32] His own *Recherches* were meant as a modest contribution to this goal: they were to serve as a manual for the *déniaisement* of his readers who risked becoming befuddled by the tendentious tales served up by the official purveyors of historical literature. Removing fantasy from the national memory and replacing it with rational conjectures founded exclusively on credible sources would serve to transform credulous readers into sharp critics, he thought.

To take one example: kings were not to be revered without reservations. They were men like other men. Even the most celebrated of them had their faults. Charlemagne, Pasquier assures his readers, on the authority of authentic sources, was given to chasing women on a grand scale.[33] Louis XI, judging from contemporary reports, did have a quick and flexible mind. He was a shrewd politician, although he was so ambitious that he spared nothing, "neither the blood nor the property of his subjects," to achieve his ends. He gave "the impression of being a pious soul, full of religion," but he used religion for his own purposes, believing, by means of "an admirable form of superstition," that there need be no limit to his excesses, as long as he made up for them by going on a pilgrimage.[34]

Such sober appraisals of the psychology of kings provoked the ire of those who would rise to "the defense of our kings against the outrages, calumnies and other impertinences of master Pasquier."[35] As for Pasquier's evaluation of the politics of the Roman Church, it was even more controversial. Writing from the point of view of a liberal Catholic, Pasquier, "speaking only as a historian," confesses that "he cannot quite convince himself that it is expedient to want to uproot heresy and defend our religion by military means." He is not even sure, he writes, assuming the pose of a simple Christian perplexed by the wars of religion, "that the use of force in such matters is permissible."[36]

The Protestants, he concedes, are surely wrong. In time, their errors will become clear to all and their sect will disappear. But it is a mistake to rely on "murder, homicide and assassination" to drive out heretics. Instead, we should reform the Church, bring back its ancient dignity—and stop the practice of appointing soldiers and children to clerical benefices. Appoint honorable people of good character to these positions, banish abuses, and you will banish heresy.[37] Pasquier's Jesuit critics were not mistaken. His conciliatory tone could not hide his fundamental suspicion of the clergy, whose rôle in politics, he observed, was to incite mobs to violence and to threaten the stability of the State. It is clear to the reader that Pasquier does not consider popes holy, that for him, "speaking only as a historian," they are simply corrupt politicians. This was already the case in Charlemagne's time, when Pope and Emperor agreed to divide the spoils (*partager le gasteau*).[38]

The bloodthirsty behavior of preachers in his own time was not a new departure either. The history of the Crusades had already provided similar examples. Embittered by the violence of Catholic zealots, Pasquier, on occasion, is prepared to condemn the entire clerical profession. "Under the false pretense of serving God, their tongues are for sale," he points out. At times "preachers have no religion other than that which suits them." Their hypocrisy, he notes bitterly, knows no bounds. "You will hear nothing coming out of their mouths except denunciations of Machiavelli, yet there is not one among those preachers who is not himself truly machiavellian, if by machiavellian we mean a preacher paid by a great lord to incite the people to join his party." The tragic consequence of the venality of unscrupulous monks, friars, and priests is that "the unfortunate populace is led by the ears, because of their simplicity, which soon can turn to rage."[39]

Such comments, in Garasse's estimation, provided clear proof of Pasquier's enmity toward the Catholic religion, perhaps toward all religion. What Garasse failed to take into account was the abyss that separated the cultural atmosphere of the 1550s, in which Pasquier's perceptions took shape, from that of the 1620s, in which Garasse was reaching prominence, making a career of denouncing *beaux-esprits*. In that earlier era, before the wars of religion, scornful comments on the behavior of unreformed monks were hardly unusual. Magistrates like La Boëtie or Pasquier, more at home in classical Rome than in the streets of Paris, tended to be suspicious of religious orders, banishing the new Society of Jesus on several occasions.

Those who belonged to Pasquier's circle tended to be wary of royal prerogatives as well when those were pressed too far. Pasquier's friend Guy du Faur de Pibrac, a respected judge and an intellectual who had been a classmate of Pasquier's at the Collège de Presles, was often cited for his philosophical verse, including the line: "*Je hays ces mots de puissance absolue.*" Montaigne and La Boëtie, both of whom were opposed to the zealotry which drove the sectarian conflict, were fairly typical of that class of humanist magistrates who set the tone in the sixteenth century. For them, religious beliefs were private matters which should not be allowed to interfere in politics or in private relationships. Pasquier maintained close friendships, throughout his long life, with magistrates, lawyers, and scholars, many of whom left the kingdom at one time or another, as Ramus had done, fearing persecution for their less than orthodox religious views.

The habit of rational argument acquired in their school years marked the humanist-educated political class on the eve of the civil wars. Urging mod-

eration, they were appalled by the breakdown of order and the frenzy of violence which followed the death of Henri II. Half a century later, Garasse's
paranoid style and extravagant accusations had become the norm. Garasse
was no fool. He knew how to inspire fear and loathing, but he was also a
competent humanities teacher who knew something, from first-hand experience, about the seductive charms of pagan learning. He was acutely aware of
the danger to his cause if Pasquier's "party of reason" should prevail.

Garasse's target was not heresy as such. The Protestant challenge was no
longer a major threat to Catholic interests in France. The new—and far
deeper—danger, as Garasse defined it, was subtler and more insidious. It proceeded, he tells his readers, from a new breed of wily opponents whose
personification was to be found in the late master Pasquier.

Who were these dangerous men? Garasse refers to them as "*libertins,*"
giving the word a new definition. "By the word *libertin*, I do not mean a
Huguenot, nor do I mean an atheist, not a Catholic either, nor a heretic, not
even a *politique*, but a certain amalgam of all these qualities. It rests on a
Catholic foundation."[40]

This new breed of which Pasquier had been, according to Garasse, the
most perfect specimen, is made up of dangerously emancipated men who
were expert at fooling the public. They would claim to be good Catholics,
but in the same breath they would add that, of course, they could hardly be
expected "to believe in all those silly notions with which priests keep the
simple people happy."[41] These *libertins*, resisting the teaching of the Church
and dead set against the religious life, will proclaim the excellence of married
life, disdaining celibacy. They will criticize the Papacy for seizing temporal
power. They will say admiring things about arch-heretics like Calvin. They
will state that it is a barbaric custom to punish people for their religious
beliefs. They will deplore the Holy Inquisition's "cannibalistic cruelty."[42]

All of these opinions were held by Pasquier, to be sure, and by many of
his friends and colleagues. What Garasse is defining, quite accurately, is the
mind set of the *philosophes*, which had been dominant in the higher reaches
of French society in the 1550s, before the civil wars, at a time when even the
most exalted Princes of the French Church, men like Cardinal de Tournon
and the Cardinal de Lorraine, were still open-minded enough to be mistaken
for "capital enemies of Ignorance."

In those early days, when Pasquier and Montaigne were young, the adoption of classical attitudes concerning religious toleration or the rights of individuals was not seen as threatening to one's faith and identity as a Christian.
Take a perfectly ordinary classics teacher, like Jean Descaurres, who had been
on the fringes of Ronsard's and Dorat's circles at the time, and had gone on to
teach school in Amiens, where he acquired a local reputation as "the Socrates

of Picardy," and eventually published a collection of his personal reflections in 1584. Even though he was by then a priest and a canon of Amiens cathedral, the *philosophe* of his youth is still obviously in charge of his way of thinking. Perfectly banal, when set in their historical context, that is to say, in the exuberant and experimental Latin Quarter of the 1550s, Descaurres' opinions, had they reached Father Garasse's desk in 1622, would have appeared to be of a piece with the outlook of the arch-*libertin*, Pasquier.

To a man such as Garasse, who loved "noble executions" and called for the most dreadful punishments to be applied to *libertins*,[43] Descaurres' insistence on condemning torture as "a cruel and inhuman practice" would have been a sure sign of his guilt,[44] since only true *libertins* would side with condemned atheists. Like Pasquier, Descaurres had no confidence in the *vulgaire*, the unfortunate and ignorant masses whose lack of discernment was well attested to by the *optimi auctores* and confirmed from direct observation. In true *libertin* fashion, Descaurres puts his trust only in the judgment of the select few.[45] This elitism is one of the distinguishing marks of the *libertin*, according to Garasse, who claims to have no problem with the opinions of the multitude and who rejects the "narrow path of reason" chosen by his opponents in favor of the "*grand chemin battu*" of public opinion.[46]

It was Pasquier—not Descaurres, not Montaigne, not Ramus—who served Garasse's purposes best. It was Pasquier's "impertinence" in presuming to judge the actions of the Kings of France that provided Garasse with his most stinging accusations. "That a subject should have the audacity of thinking, of saying, of writing that his King was silly—or given to silly ventures and notions—that is so arrogant and inappropriate a thing to say . . . that it should be punished.[47]

What makes Pasquier stand out as the standard-bearer of the *libertins* is that, unlike Montaigne, for instance, he was not hiding behind a fashionable skepticism according to which nothing could be known with certainty. Instead, every page of his *Recherches* contains documentary proof of his conjectures. It is this systematic claim to the possession of an infallible method for "ocular demonstrations" that sent Garasse into a panic. Pasquier had gone so far, in his faith in the historical method, as to claim that it should be possible in principle to predict the fate of nations with proofs as convincing as "mathematical demonstrations."[48]

Pasquier's systematic appeal to manuscript sources leaves Garasse perplexed and furious. The idea that historians should do more than copy and embellish each others' accounts is foreign to the Jesuit controversialist. Why go out of your way to contradict official chroniclers, why believe some dusty old manuscript? Why question the authenticity of the Donation of Constantine? What is the end result of taking issue with well-established sto-

ries? "When you are telling some important story taken from Moses or
Xenophon or Caesar . . . an *impertinent* will tell you coolly: "this is false, you
are mistaken, it is not as you say," and refer you to some ridiculous manuscript or other. "An *impertinent*, when you tell him that you read such and
such a thing in Pliny, will stop you short and say: have you been there? I have.
I can speak of it as an eyewitness, it is a very beautiful city."[49]

Obviously, Garasse was not interested in *"demonstrations oculaires."* He
could as easily have convicted Pierre Belon as Estienne Pasquier of impertinence, but Belon was murdered two generations earlier and had never been a
man of substance. Pasquier, on the other hand, died only recently and he had
been a powerful official and an influential and much-admired writer. He made
a far more inviting target, especially since he had always been known as an
implacable adversary of the Society of Jesus—a new religious order founded
in Rome and obedient to foreign interests. To convict Pasquier, even posthumously, of harboring deeply subversive motives was to put the spotlight on all
those who flirted with impertinence—a dangerous inclination, nowadays,
Garasse reminds his enemies. Criticizing kings is a dangerous business and
many an author guilty of such impertinence "has paid for it with his life."[50]
In sum, "freedom of expression (*liberté d'escrire et de parler*) when it is used to
criticize the sacred person of our kings, ought to be punished in an exemplary
way."[51]

What is at issue for Garasse is not the veracity of historical accounts, but
simply the respect owed to crowned heads. Needless to say, this is not a firm
principle with him or with his fellow Jesuits who had, after all, frequently
called for the assassination of Henri III and of Elizabeth I, among others.
Garasse's voluble and savage rantings are merely means of gaining support at
Court and in the streets. The fear of historical criticism, however, is a serious
matter. He returns to it again and again. As with "the bizarre ideas of
Copernicus,"[52] Pasquier's faith in the power of obscure manuscript sources
presents a fundamental challenge to established knowledge. If Pasquier is to
be believed, then all these "important stories" that sustain one's confidence
and self-esteem suddenly become worthless.

Against this mortal threat, Garasse has few defenses to offer except more
"noble executions." His trump card consists of showing that Pasquier is far
from neutral and that he has a hidden agenda, that of a cursed *libertin*, determined to sully the reputations of Christian monarchs. Again and again, in
the course of his obsessive, thousand page tract, Garasse notes that Pasquier is
assuming a position which removes him from allegiance to Rome.

Would a good Catholic entitle a chapter: "How God has made fools
both of Catholics and Huguenots"? Only a *libertin* would compose such a
chapter heading, which implies that God is not backing either side. When

Pasquier reaches the bitter conclusion that "these two sects have entirely ruined the kingdom," Garasse points out that this is not the language of a Catholic writer. To describe the Catholic Church as a sect is odious, he exclaims, and to blame both parties implies that the author does not belong to either of them, that he is, therefore, to be thought of as belonging to a third party: "He is a *libertin*, not on one side or the other."[53]

This "amphibious spirit"[54] that marks Pasquier's perspective may be detected in almost anything he wrote, according to his critic. At every turn of the page, Pasquier reveals himself to the discerning reader. What does he have to say about the massacre of Protestants on St. Bartholomew's Eve? He calls it "a barbaric cruelty."[55] What more is needed to conclude that Pasquier should have been severely punished, that agreeing with him is a certain sign of subversion, that books such as the *Recherches* should not be allowed to circulate?

Having exposed the arch-fiend, Garasse is ready to threaten any and all who might be tempted to embrace Pasquier's outlook. "*Esprits libertins*," he thunders, "your game is up, it will end in your death." This is no mere figure of speech. Garasse played a part in denouncing two of the most notorious victims of the witch-hunt orchestrated by preachers against suspect intellectuals, one of whom, Vanini, was executed in 1619, the other, Fontanier, in 1621. At the time, Garasse was working on his belated indictment of the arch-*libertin* Pasquier. These were "the two noblest executions of our time," boasts Garasse, who is as uninhibited about using terror tactics as a modern-day Ayatollah.[56]

Having created considerable controversy with the publication of his book against Pasquier, Garasse went on, two years later, to write a more ambitious treatise in which he analyzed the "curious ideas of the intellectuals of our time."[57] He was becoming a specialist in ferreting out the secret motives of the *philosophes*, *beaux-esprits*, *bons-esprits*, and assorted *libertins*. In this new book he takes the position that a crisis of unheard of proportions threatens France, threatens the Roman Church, threatens the very foundations of Christian civilization. "Atheism is slipping into the imagination of a number of souls too freely curious," he tells his readers.[58] For the benefit of those innocent souls who cannot read between the lines and who fail to see where the detachment and the irony of the *beaux-esprits* will lead, Garasse sets out to call the bluff of his enemies.

In the same spirit, his colleague, Father Mersenne, speaks of the *libertins*, who defend religious toleration and who shed tears over the fate of men strangled and burned for their religious opinions. What they really believe is that the choice of religious doctrines is a matter of profound indifference. "They judge no one and they believe that each of us will be saved, no matter what his religion may be, the Turk as well as the Jew or the Protestant."[59]

Mersenne is more specifically concerned with the damage caused by philosophy among academics. He perceives a drift toward a lukewarm Deism espoused by the intellectuals or *beaux-esprits*. "It is enough to believe in God, all the rest is human invention," is the motto of these *philosophes*, according to Mersenne.[60] Born a Frenchman, a Christian, baptized and confirmed in the Catholic Church, "a Deist of this kind will confess that, as he reached adulthood," he came to understand that religion served only to "keep simple people in check." Those whose minds have been *déniaisé*, the Deist will claim, do not need to be held in check by the fear of hell or other such intentions. They know how to act virtuously on their own, without hope of reward, without fear of retribution.[61]

Mersenne's and Garasse's reports on the state of mind of the *beaux-esprits* seem reasonably convincing. Mersenne sees a clear line of influence extending from the teaching of Ramus' time to that of his own. These were not matters to be taken lightly. Mersenne, who had good contacts in the academic world, sensed the depth of the disaffection. René Descartes was not the only student fated to put all things in doubt. Mersenne, perhaps more so than his irascible *confrère*, Garasse, feels helpless. All he can think of, to counter the arguments of the Democritic ironists, is to propose the writing of an "encyclopedia in favor of all the truths."[62]

In the meantime, like Garasse, he contents himself with threats. Addressing the nameless college teachers who introduce their students to the damnable ideology of the *philosophes*, Mersenne reminds them that the fires are burning, ready to consume them.[63] His colleagues of the Theology Faculty of the University of Paris were, at that very moment, prevailing upon the judicial authorities to publish a law which provided for the death penalty for anyone who would take it upon himself to criticize Aristotle.

The theologians and the polemical preachers were participants in a grim drama which was of a piece with the farcical atmosphere at Court in the 1620s, filled, as it was, with poisoners and necromancers, murder and mayhem. For all their shrillness, men like Mersenne and Garasse should be given credit for knowing their enemy. His intemperate style notwithstanding, Garasse had no equal as an observer of *libertins*. His summation of their philosophy, written from the perspective of a zealous defender of traditional values, is absolutely accurate. He has the *bons-esprits* or *philosophes* define their credo in their own words, emphasizing their arrogance: "They alone know how to think clearly," they say. "The mass of mankind, *les sots*, are not capable of understanding their ideas." Garasse understands the importance of science as a component of the *philosophes'* creed: "we are endowed with such curiosity that we work at unravelling Nature's secrets," he has the *libertins* boast. Perfectly attuned to the clichés favored by writers such as La Boëtie, Garasse has his *libertins* announce that they are "ready to shake off the heavy yoke of superstition which keeps the minds of men arrested in an infantile and dependent state." Sounding like Immanuel Kant, Garasse's composite free thinker explains that "it is because of superstition that we lack the courage to examine what we are told. Instead, we follow tradition and we allow ourselves to be led like oxen, with our minds closed. In this way, we are condemned to keep parroting trifles in perpetuity, in a bigoted and pedantic way, like children fearing the master's whip."[64]

6

Optimi Auctores

GARASSE AND HIS COLLEAGUES were not mistaken: college students were attracted to the *philosophes'* point of view. In fear of this development, the clergy produced a stream of warnings against the subversive effects of higher education. Close down all those colleges, ran their argument, and divert the funds to the establishment of academies reserved for the children of the nobility. The advantage of such a policy would be to redirect the energies of commoners to useful endeavors: let them stick to commerce and industry.

"Learning makes people more daring and less obedient," argued one anonymous pamphleteer, thus reaching a conclusion La Boëtie reached long ago. "The Turk is absolute," insisted the pamphlet's author admiringly. "The Turk controls his subjects perfectly, because they are illiterate." It stands to reason that if the King of France wanted to have obedient subjects in these troubled times, he should order schools closed, providing instruction only for the privileged classes. It is a well-known fact, after all, that "whoever sticks his nose in a book becomes, from that moment on, incapable of any other activity. Any villager who has learned to write three words of Latin stops paying taxes."[1]

That it was the phenomenal expansion of municipal colleges in France that was the source of the cultural shift which frightened Garasse is not be doubted.[2] One may concede that much to the redoubtable controversialist without necessarily embracing his hallucinatory vision of atheism triumphant. Reading Lucian, Horace, Seneca, Plato, or Cicero was not an unfailing recipe for turning God-fearing Christian boys into agents of Satan—but read these authors they did; they were the *optimi auctores*, the best authors, those at the very core of the Parisian style which even the Jesuits were obliged to adopt.[3]

In spite of Father Mersenne's frantic worries, the Parisian style, as practiced in some two hundred schools since the 1540s, led only exceptionally to authentic Deism, not to mention Atheism, even though it depended on the study of pagan authors exclusively. Students could perfectly well admire Horace—and pray sincerely in the college chapel on the same morning.

Jesuit polemicists tended to focus on the dangers to Christian faith contained in the curriculum, but, if anything, religious sensibilities were more thoroughly insulated from the unsettling consequences of higher education than were other, less easily defined attitudes. Garasse was perspicacious enough, at odd moments, to note that the disease he was diagnosing was not transmitted by means of challenges to Christian doctrine alone; at the heart of the malaise, he discovered, there was to be found a coherent and seductive ideology whose axioms were grounded in what appeared to be historical—or pseudo-historical—reflections.

In the beginning, said the *philosophes*, there was a Golden Age, when we lived in accordance with Nature's precepts. In those days, our ancestors were happy. They could not imagine theft, mistrust, or greed. None were rich, none were poor. The very idea that a portion of the earth could be declared someone's private property, such a notion, with its concomitant incitement to envy, did not exist as yet, any more than it exists among the newly discovered populations of the Americas. Needless to say, there was no conceivable opportunity for tyrants, dictators, or kings to exist in such a world. There was no need for laws, for lawyers, for beggars or convicts. Just like the tribes inhabiting the coasts of Brazil, or the islanders Columbus encountered in the Caribbean, our ancestors led easy, guileless lives.

At some point, alas—most likely when someone, for the first time, thought of shouting: this land is mine!—the original liberty and equality Nature endowed us with began to give way, in the course of a long apprenticeship, to the detestable condition we call civilization. Clear-eyed observers of this development should be in a position to bring back the essential features of our ancestors' paradisiac existence. This, in a nutshell, was the ideology of the *philosophes*.

Could it be fairly described as a threat to Christianity? Only by preachers determined to see one more monstrous foe rising to challenge them, in the wake of Luther's heresy, and of the demonic activities of Jews and witches, those categories of miscreants taunting overworked inquisitors. From the perspective of the defenders of orthodoxy, the "bizarre ravings of Copernicus," the dangerous teaching of Galileo or the blasphemous notions of Bruno were all part of a gigantic conspiracy designed to undermine eternal verities. As for those elegant and nonchalant *beaux-esprits*, what was that philosophy of theirs, hidden behind ironic smiles? It was pure paganism, and of the worst sort, masquerading as humanitarian tolerance while subverting the entire edifice of Christian morality.

Garasse understood that it was liberty that was at the heart of the *philosophes'* outlook—liberty as opposed to obedience. His choice of a word with which to describe the self-styled *philosophes* or *bons-esprits* is not inaccurate: they were *libertins*. While Garasse asks only to follow the Church's every command without question and considers it sheer folly to express judgments about one's natural superiors, the *libertins* refuse to submit to anyone's judgment and refuse to grant that kings were their God-given masters. To men such as Garasse or Mersenne, members of religious communities trained to suppress their individual wills, the mental universe of someone like Pasquier was disturbing in the extreme. By what right did the *beaux-esprits* claim to be free of the restrictions that governed the lives of ordinary, dutiful Christians? In what sense could they be considered Christians at all? They swore only by their pagan mentors and ignored the most fundamental of Christian doctrines, including that of original sin and of the immortality of the soul. They set up their own morality which was at odds with that of the Church.

To pinpoint the radical nature of the *philosophes'* challenge, Mersenne singles out the dangerous ideas of a most popular writer, Pierre Charron, who was himself a priest and the author of a widely read *Book of Wisdom*.[4] Charron's wisdom was not compatible with the wisdom of Mersenne. In typical *philosophe* fashion, Charron expressed his contempt for the *sotte multitude*, paraphrasing Horace and calling the mass of the people "a strange beast with several heads," as inconstant "as the waves of the sea," credulous and lacking in judgment. In sum, "*le vulgaire est une beste sauvage*."[5] Charron speaks of virtue in a way which is openly in contradiction with the theologians' definition. Their virtue, says Charron, is "austere, sad, fearful, full of chagrin, slavish and common." The virtue of the *philosophe*, he tells us, is quite the opposite: it is "gay, free, joyous, uncommon, humorous," strong, as well, and noble, generous and rare. He is not "preparing men for the cloister," explains Charron, "but for the world."[6]

It was the independence of mind of the *philosophes* that enraged their opponents. Charron expresses himself, in his *Sagesse*, very much in the way of Talon, Ramus, or Tahureau. "They may believe that I can be swayed by authoritative pronouncements, that I will accept a legion of other men's allegations," he writes. "All this carries very little weight with me—except in matters of religion," he adds prudently. "I should believe everything the ancients said? And everything the common people believe? Only idiots will allow themselves to be led in this way. The wise man, the *philosophe*, is above the laws, by right, even though he will make an effort, in public, to obey them." Cherishing his "*liberté d'esprit*," the *philosophe* will refuse to subject his mind "to any kind of servitude." He allows "neither his passions nor public opinion to deprive him of the freedom to see, to judge, to examine all things." He always reaches his own conclusions, although he will not "oblige anyone else to share them."[7]

Charron is especially sharp in his analysis of the hypocrisy of those who, under cover of piety, pretend to lead virtuous lives belied by their actions. "Angels in Church, Devils at home," such persons practice "little external devotions" obsessively, without being any better for all that. "They disguise impious thoughts with the appearance of piety, they make a business and a profession of their piety."[8] Those who are concerned only with religion "do not recognize any virtue other than that which is set into action by the mechanism of religion," writes Charron severely. He does not have much faith in those who act virtuously only out of fear of eternal punishment. He much prefers the person who does good without expecting to enter Paradise.[9] Virtue should come first, religion should be "posterior," that is, a natural consequence of a person's virtue. There are, after all, "religious persons who are evil and irreligious *philosophes* who are virtuous.[10]

Charron's *Sagesse* was an obvious target of militant traditionalists in the 1620s. The book is usually understood to be a distillation of Montaigne's *Essays*. More to the point, both Charron and his admired mentor, Montaigne, were writing handbooks for virtuous living which summed up the wisdom of the *optimi auctores*. The cultural revolution which made Garasse and his colleagues so uneasy had no other source than the classroom. Garasse, himself a teacher, knew this perfectly well. The entire strategy of the Jesuit order, from the very beginning of its appearance in France, was devised as a counterattack against the secular teachers of the Parisian style. Fighting fire with fire, the Jesuits adopted the *modus parisiensis* and hoped to teach the *optimi auctores* without inflicting moral harm to their charges.[11]

The dangers that impressionable young minds were exposed to in the classroom can be summed up easily enough. Before the 1520s, only a few of the books that were to acquire the generic descriptive label of "classics"—that is, of the classroom—had been available for teaching purposes. The academic publishing industry, prodded by the zeal of Erasmian scholars, introduced a revolution in learning habits. The very goals of education were redefined. No longer "teaching for the cloister," and preparing instead "to shape a man for the world," as Charron was to put it, the college teachers following the Parisian style had no use for the scholastic logic that had customarily been parceled out to aspiring theologians. Contemptuous of medieval textbooks and commentaries, which struck them as awkward and far removed from the true sources of *bonae literae*, they were persuaded that all true learning was to be found in the *optimi auctores* directly. They were ready to jettison all the commentaries and glosses produced in the past thousand years and return to the sources, *ad fontes*.

Their students were expected to achieve fluency in the reading of the classical languages, and a certain ease in the writing of correct—that is, Ciceronian—Latin. Such skills were not to be learned from clerical tutors. The colleges turned to newer specialists, men such as Lambin or Muret, who were at home in the world of the *auctores*, who could read Plato and Plutarch in the original—and who could teach their students to compose odes and epigrams, even entire stage-worthy tragedies modeled after classical originals.

Even before Ramus established his demonstration school in 1548, the demand for the new style of schooling was felt everywhere in the kingdom. The establishment of a municipal college at Bordeaux in 1533 was not the earliest example of the Parisian style exported to satellite locations, but it was the most ambitious. As a case study of the rupture with the medieval clerical model of education, the events in Bordeaux are especially revealing. There had been a university here, founded by papal charter in 1446. Lodged in a convent, it had a faculty of six theologians, two teachers of canon law, two teachers of civil law, and two masters of arts. Occasionally a professor of medicine is mentioned as well.[12] In 1486, responsibility for the university was assumed by the mayor and the city council of Bordeaux. As of that moment, the university ceased to be a clerical institution. It was pressed into service to suit the needs of the bourgeois of Bordeaux, who were paying for the institution's functioning with their taxes.

The elected officials of Bordeaux inherited a "university" which amounted to little more than a collection of clerical sinecures. Not much teaching went on in that convent, nor was there much demand for courses in theology and canon law among the bourgeois of Bordeaux. What they wanted was a college of liberal arts in the Parisian style. To accomplish this objective, the city immediately bought two properties near city hall for future use as classroom space. Ignoring the theologians and canon lawyers, the city council developed a long-term strategy for housing a large college that would take in young children and provide efficient instruction in the classics for however long it would take to master the *optimi auctores*. The first requirement was to make the books available. For this purpose, the city hired a German printer, in the summer of 1486, who was to supply the new school's needs. More space would be needed as well. At first, the students were housed in four "small, damp and dark dwellings" (*petites, acquatiques et tenebreuses maisons*). A fifth house was eventually rented, in 1519, and further additions were made in 1525, as the college was bursting at the seams, so great was the demand. At last, on February 22, 1533, the city signed a contract with a Parisian college principal: he was to hire twenty instructors, bring them to Bordeaux, and establish a full-scale college on the Parisian model.[13]

The contract focused on the material aspects of this gargantuan project: 336 out-of-town students were to be lodged as boarders in new dormitories. Eleven houses would be needed for 15 classrooms, two study halls, 26 rooms for lodging the staff. An auditorium was to be built, a dining hall and a chapel would be required and a separate building as well, to house the classrooms of the younger children. All in all, an entire city block, acquired bit by bit after 1486, was needed to house the college which would eventually be enrolling more than 2000 students, according to a recent estimate. The cost to the city in salaries alone was to be 500 livres each year.[14] This contract was not just a project: the college actually opened its doors on May 24, 1533.

Dazzled by the Rabelaisian dimensions of this venture, we might easily miss the most radical changes introduced at Bordeaux. These concern what is taught and how it is taught and who does the teaching. Simply put: the Renaissance had come to town. The new masters recruited in Paris were classics teachers who, like Peter Ramus, were more in tune with Budé and Erasmus than with the Sorbonne establishment. And quite a few of these masters were serious scholars well known in humanist circles, including Cordier, Buchanan, and Muret. The curriculum was a straightforward progression in the Latin classics. Greek was taught as well. And so was mathematics.

How could this be done on so large a scale? The answer is: by introducing the system of graduated classes to replace the tutorial system. Instead of being attached to a single master from the start of his education to the finish, the student in the new system moves from one class up to the next one, as he masters the subject or drops out. Each master is a specialist. Beginners are under the care of the *abecedaire*, who teaches reading skills. Once he can read, in Latin and French, the student graduates to the next level where he studies simple and short texts taken from classical sources. Year by year he works his way up from the Sixth to the First Form.

The new municipal college was an efficient factory for turning out young Latinists. The kind of competence expected was much higher than that required of earlier students and the course was considerably longer: it took ten years to complete it. This was not a preparatory course for future theologians. It was designed as a complete education.[15]

An able student like Michel Eyquem, better known in later years as Monsieur de Montaigne, entered the Bordeaux College at the age of 6, in 1539. He completed his classes seven years later, in 1546, at the age of 13 or 14. The college allowed a thoughtful and precocious teenager who had completed the most advanced class to stay right on in his accustomed lodgings. He could continue his education informally by attending public lectures in Greek and mathematics offered by the most expert of the masters, usually the principal himself. The student was largely on his own at this point. Young Montaigne studied with the hellenist Grouchy, and perhaps with George Buchanan as well and the 21-year-old philologist Marc Antoine Muret, in whose play, *Julius Caesar*, Montaigne acted a part in 1547, the year following his formal completion of the most advanced class.

This last stage of an education in the provincial colleges is not easy to define. It took the place of the obligatory three-and-a-half-year philosophy course in Paris on which Peter Ramus wasted his youth. It was called philosophy—or, more loosely, *liberae auscultationes* (informal auditing) and it involved two years of residence at Bordeaux. There was probably no uniform way of pursuing these post-graduate studies, which permitted the granting of a master's degree.[16] Montaigne did not need a degree. Presumably he wanted to keep up his studious habits, his friendships, his conversations with learned men, his browsing in bookstores, his flirtations. All this could be done better in Paris.

Roger Trinquet may be right in thinking that Montaigne spent some time in Paris after he had exhausted the cultural resources of Bordeaux. Buchanan and Muret were already back in Paris. Their 17-year-old protégé could have dropped in on the public lectures of the royal professors, including those of Peter Ramus. In the literary salons of Paris, the young provincial could have met classicists like Adrien Turnèbe and all sorts of clever and erudite young men and women.[17] He could also have attended the lectures of fashionable jurists, in spite of the fact that the University of Paris did not officially have a civil law faculty.[18] All this would have been quite informal. Indeed Montaigne probably never studied law formally. There was no need: his education was complete. And it had been completed entirely within the world of the humanist liberal arts college.

Wherever there was some remnant of a medieval university in a French city, with the exception of Paris, the municipal authorities took over the institution and remade the Arts Faculty into an ambitious humanist college. They did away with the tutorial system and replaced it with the class system, which was standardized and modular in nature. That is to say that a Troisième or a Sixième, anywhere, was just about the same, requiring the same textbooks and the same teaching methods. It had to be that way, because the masters of arts hired to teach were often brought in at the last minute and they were likely to be gone when their contract was up the following year. They had to fit right in.

The profile of the teaching profession changed quickly. Instead of tenured and vaguely clerical *pauvres perpetuels*, still the dominant strain in Paris, we find young *pères de famille* in the provinces, married or hoping to be so, salaried and on one year contracts. The city councils naturally imprinted the norms of the bourgeois on their colleges. They did not expect anyone to do good work unless he was paid according to his merit and his usefulness. And they distrusted celibacy. Hence the word would go out, in Aix-en-Provence for instance, that the city intended to hire five "decent, experienced, and well-married masters."[19]

The successful creation of a new model of education was part of a nationwide pattern, although only some cities, in the 1530s and 1540s, could afford a full-scale college in the style of Paris, with as many as six different *professores* or *régents*, each responsible for his own class. To offer instruction in Greek as well as in Latin literature, to teach mathematics and to adopt a uniform set of standards, allowing students to be examined for proficiency at regular intervals—all this required considerable expenditures. Add to this the cost of subsidizing a printer and bookseller and the expense of regular searches when recruiting new instructors every fall term, and it is not surprising to see a number of cities improvising, with uneven results, while waiting to resolve the financial and administrative difficulties they were facing.

Here and there, smaller cities such as Grenoble or Nevers thought they could manage by hiring just one or two highly recommended classicists instead of going all out like opulent Bordeaux. Grenoble hired the 24-year-old Hubert Sussaneau, in 1536, to direct the municipal school. Sussaneau, a friend of Rabelais, had been preparing editions of Cicero and Horace for the Lyon publisher Gryphius. He took the job in Grenoble and stayed for several years, but he was fired, eventually, on the ground that he was setting a bad example. He was said to be ill-tempered and erratic in his teaching. "He would start teaching one book, abandon it after two or three chapters, and go on to another book altogether." Meanwhile he would scandalize those around him by his wild behavior, swearing loudly, "blaspheming against God," and drunk, as well, most of the time. He carried a sword and was prepared to fight any and all.[20]

Such experiences were not uncommon. By 1554, Grenoble came a step closer to setting up a permanent and respectable college. That year, the city's chief executive, the First Consul, traveled to Paris on an official mission. He was accompanied by the current school principal. While in Paris, the two men discussed their city's educational needs and reached the conclusion that it was a mistake to put all their eggs in one basket in the hope of recruiting a single, exceptionally wide-ranging scholar who would teach all the humanities classes and Greek and philosophy as well. Since their arrival in Paris, as they surveyed various possibilities and tested the job market for classics teachers, the two officials had come to realize that the demand for competent instructors was so high that their hope of finding an exceptional combination of skills "in one person, especially a person willing to leave Paris to travel so far for a salary of 100 livres," was unrealistic.

The two envoys decided to recommend the hiring of two instructors to replace a single man. They had candidates in mind. "One of them taught philosophy in Reims, the other is a good Greek scholar who can also teach the humanities." Doubling the school's annual salary expenditures, they suggested that 200 livres would do, for both men, although an advance should be offered to help with travel expenses. To be sure, added the First Consul, money would be hard to find, but, in his opinion, the expenditure was worth considering, "so as to provide our youth with the only true inheritance, which is knowledge."[21]

Evidently a great many consuls, aldermen, and mayors in other French cities felt that way. Between 1529 and 1558, most of them joined the great rush for equipping cities with proper schools in the Parisian style. The example of the city of Moulins is entirely typical in this respect. In 1529, Moulins was getting along with a single schoolmaster who taught in a house rented by the city for this purpose. Three years later, the city was recruiting in Paris, probably without success. In 1533, they were able to hire a teacher from Lyon. "Let him come just as quickly as possible and let us provide a comfortable house for him," recommended the city councilors, imbued, as they were, with a sense of urgency. A year later the city had two teachers and in 1539 they had expanded the school to a staff of three. At this point the city took the big step of investing 700 livres and buying a house for the school. By 1552, there was a staff of 4 or 5 teachers in the school. The contract signed by the principal on April 27, 1556, provides for 200 livres in salaries and a staff of five, allowing the school in Moulins, now referred to as a college, to function "like those in Paris."[22]

The enthusiasm for public education was so high and so widely shared in the sixteenth century that the municipal colleges rarely charged tuition to residents and always welcomed the children of "honest families who cannot afford to pay such fees and whose sons will some day become *gens de bien*." On the assumption that high-level schooling benefits the entire community, city councils were willing to divert rare resources to their new public colleges.

Even truly small towns, such as Condom, in Gascony, went ahead and shifted funds originally assigned to other purposes, such as poor relief. The college at Condom was to have a staff of seven eventually. Considering the size of the town and its tax base, this would appear very ambitious indeed. The proponents of college expansion admitted this, but argued that theirs was "a holy project." They assured the citizens of Condom that, "where there is learning, the *république* profits." Carried away by his own rhetoric, the official who headed the drive spoke of the urgency of this matter: "we have to move fast, no matter what the cost," he declared, because "learning (*science*) magnifies God's glory, honors the king and maintains, augments and conserves the republic." As for diverting funds earmarked for the hospital, that was all right, "since it is far more charitable to nourish mind and body together, rather than the body alone."[23]

Everywhere the demand was for the Parisian style. In Brittany, in Burgundy or in Provence, the wording of contracts with principals makes this clear. "The children of the noble bourgeois [*sic*]," say the bourgeois of Rennes, "must be taught, regulated and governed honorably and with *bonne littérature*, on the model of the Parisian colleges (*à l'exsemble des colleiges de Paris*)."[24] In time, as the colleges began to resemble each other in almost every way, since all were functioning on the same model, a regular hiring circuit came into being, with candidates for teaching positions moving from one school to another, lured by higher salaries or prospects for advancement. The textbooks used in all these colleges were standardized too, in the form of the *opera omnia* of the *optimi auctores*. Buildings, books, curriculum, staffing and expectations all crystallized by the 1550s into a system which took root so deeply that it was to prove close to indestructible when the political climate shifted and Church and State joined in an attack on the colleges of the bourgeois.

7

Dangerous Classes

WHAT HAD STARTED OUT innocently enough as a cultural revolution applauded in most quarters and seemingly irresistible in its progress soon became embroiled in a political conflict so profound that it was to divide an entire nation. Royal policy at first was entirely favorable to the establishment of new secular colleges. Why would the king oppose such worthwhile projects, especially since the cities were paying for them? The French Church, on the other hand, was suspicious. Every municipal college that opened its doors was a slap in the face of the local diocese which, until then, had been responsible for education. The fact that this responsibility had rarely been taken seriously did not deter bishops and canons from accusing city councils of usurpation of authority, especially when cities instituted legal proceedings intended to capture a portion of clerical revenues as a subsidy for the new schools.

These were serious concerns, but they were overshadowed by the clergy's mistrust of the new teachers. The very notion that laymen should teach children struck the clergy as an incomprehensible break with tradition. When the consuls of Nîmes presented their new professor, master Cavart, to the diocesan authorities in October of 1537, the bishop's agent recoiled in horror as if Cavart had just arrived from another planet. The man "was not known to him," he complained. Astounded, he observed that Cavart was not wearing clerical garments (*il n'estoit pas in habitu clericale*). Working himself up into a rage, he shouted at Cavart, ordering him to shave off his beard on pain of excommunication, a beard being the most obvious sign of lay status. Master Cavart replied, with perfect logic, stating what should have been obvious, namely that the bishop had no jurisdiction over him, since he was not a tonsured cleric. The conversation had reached a perfect dead end.[1]

The deepest fear of the clergy was that the new schools were not what they seemed and that the new teachers brought with them something besides Latin grammar. Those fears, which were eventually to be expressed in exquisite detail by Garasse or Mersenne, were only dimly articulated in the early days of the Parisian style's expansion. Almost inevitably, given the prominence of the Protestant challenge, opponents of the schools tended to accuse the teachers of heresy, a conventional crime which the authorities were equipped to deal with. And it was true, in the 1530s, that a connection existed between humanist teachers and the movement for religious reform. "All French Protestants of any importance had been taught by humanists" and, for that matter, "all the humanists, at some early stage, were in favor of religious revolution." This formulation, which belongs to Henri Hauser, may be a little too all-encompassing, but it is essentially true. What Hauser saw clearly was that, as late as 1530, the dividing line between competing dogmas was still fluid enough in France so that it is anachronistic to speak of Catholics and Protestants. "Every Christian thought of himself as Catholic, every good Christian wished to reform the Church."[2]

This was the attitude which allowed intellectuals such as Ramus to feel comfortable in their relationship to ecclesiastical patrons, and this was the climate of opinion in which bishop Du Bellay sent his protégé to study in Wittenberg and Cardinal de Tournon surrounded himself with suspect types such as Lambin, Muret, or Rondelet. It was only when lines began to harden that expressions of sympathy for reform ran the risk of being interpreted as subversion. Eventually, suspect teachers, printers and booksellers were denounced and arrested, in bursts of local vigilante fever, wherever the targets were vulnerable enough and wherever the secular authorities allowed such inquisitions to take place.[3]

The new teachers at municipal schools were almost automatically suspect. A particularly well documented case of an inquisitor on a fishing expedition among teachers and students comes from the town of Agen, southeast of Bordeaux, in March of 1537.[4] The chief target of the inquisitor's curiosity was the principal, master Philibert Sarrasin. Sarrasin had been in charge of the school at Agen for three years. As one would expect, he was an outsider, he was "not known" to the local clergy. Of Burgundian origin, he had completed his studies at a university, most likely in Paris. Although he taught classics and philosophy, he also had a medical degree. He had been brought in by the consuls of Agen to run the municipal school with the help of two other capable teachers, one a specialist in grammar, the other in the liberal arts. The budget was 100 livres a year. The school was not to charge tuition to the children of the town's residents, although the principal could collect hefty fees from out-of-town boarders.

When the inquisitor began interrogating witnesses, one of the teachers, master Pierre Allard, Sarrasin's deputy and eventual successor, came to the court's attention early on. A witness described Allard as a thin man with prominent teeth and a long red beard whom he had met a year earlier at the home of a tailor of his acquaintance. The witness was playing cards at the tailor's home that evening. Allard joined the company and stayed throughout the evening, in the course of which he was heard to say a number of things which made the other men uncomfortable. "There is no need to confess to priests," he would say, but when he noticed the discomfort of the other guests, he added: "Let's drop it, such things are not to everyone's taste."

Another witness, an older student, testified against the principal, Sarrasin, in whose company he found himself on a visit to Bordeaux, where Sarrasin was meeting with a distinguished colleague, Mathurin Cordier. According to the witness, the two teachers were discussing Luther's views on Free Will. They were standing in a church at the time and, according to the witness, Sarrasin commented on the votive candles near the altar, saying that the lighting of candles served no religious purpose, that it was a custom "inherited from eunuchs and pagans."

As witness followed witness in Agen that spring, it became clear that the habit of expressing unorthodox points of view was not the sole prerogative of Sarrasin and of Allard. The presence of these masters seemed to have resulted in the creation of a network of sympathizers. Even Sarrasin's maid, Jeanne, was in the habit of speaking her mind freely, "as if she, too, were a big-shot intellectual" (*l'on eust dit que c'estait une grande clergesse*), complained an indignant local widow who testified against her.

If one is to believe the hostile witnesses pouring out their grievances against the masters and students of the college, it would seem that the mockery practiced by the new intellectuals in town was finding echoes in many private homes. A priest testified that he was present in the home of master Nadal, the most important government official in town, when he noticed that Allard, with his flowing red beard, was present, too, acting as tutor to the Nadal children. Allard, said the priest, held a Bible in his hands and was heard making a number of unorthodox remarks. Another priest testified in similar terms against the tutor of the local doctor's children.

Among the witnesses appearing before the inquisitor, there were not only priests and widows, but also students in their twenties—perhaps preparing for clerical careers. There were master masons among the accusers and even teachers, colleagues of Sarrasin's, like master Molerat. Molerat, born in the diocese of Cahors, had a master's degree from Paris. He was about 35 years old. He testified against the principal, whom he accused of saying, in the course of a heated debate in the home of another teacher, that "*opera non sunt necessaria ad salutem*" (good works are not necessary for salvation).

Slipping out of the classrooms, arguments found their way into private homes and student boarding houses. A student who lodged in a priest's home found himself accused of making claims that the priest found shocking: he had read the Old and New Testaments in their entirety, the student claimed. This scandalous admission, which marked him as a heretic, was heard by a second priest, as well. In another boarding house, the owner, a widow, suffered from the imprudent talk of two students, the Durfort brothers, who were heard to speak against indulgences and pardons and who denied the existence of purgatory. They also said, according to the witness, that it was wrong to pray to saints, that one should pray to God alone. When the landlady protested against these enormities, the brothers laughed at her and called her "*bigotte*." The Durfort brothers had become notorious in town. A priest who had the misfortune of living in the same boarding house complained of their taunts. "Get to work, you priests, get to work," was the Durforts' refrain. They also claimed that the Pope was a man in no way different from other men, that he had no power to forgive sins.

The portrait of the unremarkable town of Agen that emerges from these interrogations is surprising. If one is to believe the many witnesses clamoring to be heard, the whole town was arguing about rather technical aspects of piety. Both the accused and the accusers were in some way linked to the college, either as teachers and students or as local *gens de bien* who maintained close relations with Sarrasin and his colleagues—or else as incensed priests and their supporters who felt deeply threatened by the freewheeling talk of the arrogant college crowd.

Something that one could not guess from official records, such as the principal's contract or minutes of city council meetings, is that bringing a reputable college in the manner of Paris to town would result in the unofficial presence of all sorts of teachers whose names appear in no contracts and who may not have been on any public payroll. Quite a few of them are mentioned in the course of the interrogations. What were they doing in town? Had they come to seek teaching posts and lost out to Sarrasin and to Allard in the competitions conducted each Fall in city hall? Were they employed, somehow, while waiting for posts to open up? Did they make some kind of living by coaching students? And what about the constant stream of visiting academics attracted by Sarrasin's reputation, who made a habit of stopping over in Agen, spending the night at the college and sharing their high-octane gossip with their hosts?

A glimpse of these goings-on is offered to the inquisitor through the testimony of the merchant Phillippe Solern. Two years earlier Sarrasin was living in Solern's home and tutoring his son Jean. There were other boys coming to Solern's home as well, to join in Sarrasin's lessons. Among these were the Durfort brothers, whose names crop up everywhere. Solern's house must have been fairly substantial, because it seems that Allard was living there also and he had two boys living with him, the sons of a Bordeaux judge. As if this astonishing concentration of bookish lodgers were not enough, "all kinds of students and teachers coming from distant lands and passing through town" made a point of stopping over at Solern's house. Other foreigners actually resided in town, even though they are not mentioned in the college contract. There was a German teacher named "Stella" (Stern?), who had the inevitable Durfort brothers lodging with him—they seemed to move around a lot—and who was also, it seems, in the habit of receiving visitors from Germany.

Agen was not Bordeaux or Lyon. Agen was an ordinary town, yet it was wide open to the currents that were sweeping through the Latin Quarter in Paris or actually bypassing dangerous Paris to move along sheltered corridors leading from towns like Nevers, where Cordier had been principal in 1529, to grander colleges like the one in Bordeaux, where Cordier was teaching in 1535 and where Sarrasin met him, and on to Geneva and Lausanne, where Cordier and Sarrasin eventually were to find refuge.[5] Calvin himself was a classics teacher on the run, at the time, making a living in Strasbourg running a student boarding house just like "Stella" in Agen. Both Bèze, Calvin's eventual lieutenant in Geneva, and Farel, who brought Calvin to the Swiss city in the first place, were college teachers by profession.

For some thirty years, before the conflict between Catholics and Protestants actively erupted into open warfare in France, the highly mobile emissaries of the Parisian style carried a good deal of dangerous contraband in their baggage. Were they Protestant missionaries? This would be far too unambiguous a conclusion.[6] Almost all the statements reported to the Inquisition in Agen belong squarely in the tradition identified with Erasmus and his disciples. To read Scripture, to pray to God directly, to scoff at the efficacy of candles, to denounce priests for their ignorance or venality, these were commonplaces amusingly inserted in the favorite schoolbooks of the new colleges, in Erasmus' and Cordier's Colloquies.

To denounce teachers as Protestants was a highly effective strategy for Catholic propagandists. There were, of course, secret Protestants to be found on college faculties, and almost everywhere one could find teachers who favored a reformed kind of piety, the kind Erasmus preached, but it was easy for a suspicious theologian to mistake a mild Erasmian anti-clericalism for authentic Calvinist or Lutheran sectarianism. Just as Eramus himself, who had been almost universally admired and favored by Pope and Emperor at one time, was to become *persona non grata* to both sides in the conflict, so the *professores classici* as a whole were to come under suspicion, in the wake of Luther's revolution. Catholics viewed them as heretics ex officio, while Protestants were quick to claim persecuted teachers as martyrs to their cause. Zealots of both persuasions were not likely to understand that theological disputes were not the chief concern of French college teachers.

Someone like Ramus, summoned to declare his theological allegiance, could not do so without doing violence to his convictions. His hopes for humanity were directed at goals that theologians of any kind would have considered suspect. Not the interpretation of the mass, or the efficacy of sacraments, but the rejection of injustice, of poverty and of repression, these were matters of deep concern to him. His proposed solution to the ills of the world was not the Second Coming, but the introduction of good thinking into the minds of the greatest possible number of his brothers.

Such objectives were not easily reconciled with the imperatives of theologians. Like Erasmus, Ramus would find himself in the unenviable position of being rejected by both sides. Assaulted and vilified by the Catholic party in Paris, he tried to find a teaching post at Protestant colleges abroad, without success. In spite of his fame, he was not welcome in the Lutheran, Calvinist, or Reformed colleges dominated by theologians. "He stands against Aristotle," was the curt reply in Strasbourg when he presented his candidacy. From Geneva, Théodore de Bèze wrote to say that there would be no vacancy at his college.

At bottom, there was not much difference between Catholic and Protestant theologians when they were confronted with a genuine maverick like Ramus. Both kinds of theologians relied on a scholastic, Aristotelian system which provided no room for independent thinking. Neither the new science of Copernicus, nor the rationalism of the ancients, unfiltered by Christian commentary, could be freely examined without a declaration of independence from dogma. It was obvious that someone as emancipated from authority as Ramus was could not be expected to pay obeisance to the new Pope of Geneva. Théodore de Bèze understood this very well when he warned his colleagues against Ramus' "democratic" tendencies."[7]

It was the common experience of college principals in many French cities to become the targets of suspicion and to be confronted by both sides in the sectarian conflicts. Neither the bishops nor the Calvinist pastors could fathom the minds of men who were not prepared to declare their allegiance to either side. Was there a third position?

The city of Nîmes provides an instructive case history in this respect. The municipal authorities were heavily engaged on the Protestant side while the bishop led the Catholic opposition. Here, as in many other cities, the battle was to be played out over the control of public schooling. By 1553 the consuls had secured the financial foundation of their ambitious college and recruited a first-rate Parisian principal, master Touffan. In spite of the respect he commanded, Touffan was soon caught up in the red-hot politics of a divided city. The bishop summoned him to "declare of what religion he was." The ministers, for their part, pressured the principal to change the college's curriculum and to tailor it to their needs. They wanted the study of the *optimi auctores* abridged in favor of the study of theology.

Touffan stood his ground. He refused to declare his religious preferences. As for the ministers' demand that he truncate the Parisian style and introduce theology at the earliest opportunity, this, too, he resisted. He wrote a letter to his employers, the consuls of Nîmes, explaining that "if the boys begin the study of theology before they are ready, I fear we will soon face the same problems our ancestors experienced, namely that, in future, ministers may be as ignorant as priests have been in the past." Raising the specter of hordes of incompetent graduates pouring out of the colleges and taking up positions as pastors in spite of their sketchy education, "lacking experience, lacking knowledge, and often lacking good character as well," Touffan resisted all attempts to turn his college into a seminary. The pressures he was exposed to prompted him to complain to the city authorities. He could not get enough sleep, he protested. He had to be on call night and day, "his mind as tense as a drawn bow." He was forced to reply to more letters than "the secretary of a great lord." He had to assume responsibility for the faults committed by his teachers, his servants, and his students. He found himself constantly in the position of having to substitute for absent or sick teachers. For that matter, it was getting so difficult to replace teachers, especially in the advanced classes, that he found himself substituting for as long as a month at a time. "And all the while, *bon Dieu*, the whole town is complaining about the lack of order in the college and the principal's poor management. Why, there isn't a boilermaker or a woolcarder in this town who doesn't claim he could do a better job!"

Touffan eventually resigned. His reluctance to continue serving the city was no isolated case, as he understood perfectly well. "As for the difficulties we are encountering in recruiting teachers, these difficulties will certainly increase in time, because the most learned teachers are leaving the profession as fast as they can." Principals, in particular, he explained, now belonged to a category of persons "subjected to more scandal" than any other. Everywhere, the principal is called "an apostate" and said to be "a traitor," in the opinion of the "*populaire*." He predicted that it would become more and more difficult to find new principals.[8]

He was right, of course. Scholarly teachers who read Plato and the New Testament in the original language and whose minds were open to the exploration of diverse and conflicting points of view, following the example of the *optimi auctores*, such men would naturally resist embracing the simplified and menacing battle cries of religious zealots. Touffan's experience in Protestant Nîmes was frustrating, but Aneau, the principal in Lyon, was lynched by a Catholic mob while Touffan was composing his letter to the consuls. Aneau was an erudite humanist active at the center of a network of intellectual friendships in this wealthy city filled with publishing houses, printers, and book-sellers. From the perspective of Catholic militants he would appear as a dangerous Protestant sympathizer. His elimination, and the defeat of the Protestant faction in Lyon, paved the way for the introduction of the Jesuits in this strategic city whose archbishop, Cardinal de Tournon, was quickly becoming the General Patton of the French Counter-Reformation.[9] Meanwhile, Calvinist ministers regarded intellectuals such as Ramus, Aneau, and Touffan with suspicion, concluding, from their apparently neutral stance, that they were apostates or traitors. There were no words available, in the vocabulary of the religious debate, for describing the position of those who could not be fitted squarely into the Catholic or Protestant camp.

The most common attitude within the teaching profession—among the secular teachers, that is—right up to the 1560s was to accept, at least outwardly, the religious attitudes of the majority in the towns they served. Outward Catholics for the most part, they were inclined, at the same time, to accept much of the Reformers' criticisms of traditional practices. It seemed reasonable to them that the Pope was a man like any other, and thus could hardly be expected to act like God, forgiving individual sins, or like God's banker, selling pardons. The most common attitude encountered among the philosophical spokesmen of the Parisian style was a cautious neutrality founded on the notion that religion was a private matter which was not directly relevant to the study of grammar and that one should avoid massacring neighbors whose intimate religious convictions did not match one's own.

In many French towns there were families, usually the majority, which remained loyal to the Church of Rome, and others which chose to join the Reformed Church. Was it any business of the teaching staff, in a public school, to take sides? Was it not desirable that teachers should distance themselves from religious politics? It was in this spirit that a modest schoolteacher, master Raymond Chaussenc, applied for a position in the small town of Le Buis, in the foothills east of the Rhône valley. Writing to the town's consuls, he explained that he had heard that their schoolmaster was leaving. Chaussenc offered his services to the consuls. Listing his qualifications, the candidate writes: "I am willing to serve you and teach your children good *moeurs*, as well as reading in Latin and French." As an added inducement, he points out that he has "a wife who is not staying with me at the moment." He is prepared to send for his wife who can teach the girls reading, writing, and good *moeurs* and who "is as good at this work as any that can be found in the entire province."

There is just one slight problem, he acknowledges. "I happen to be a Protestant. This may create some difficulty for those of you who are Catholic. But I beg you to fear nothing, because I am used to teaching Catholic children in such a way that you will never know that I am a Protestant, as you will be able to verify when you hire me."[10]

Such finely calibrated attitudes were not uncommon, even though an upsurge of street violence and the victory of the Catholic party, which could take the form of an assault at gunpoint against the public college, made the position of ecumenically minded teachers precarious. Principals of Touffan's kind were becoming an endangered species. In spite of a number of experiments in peaceful cohabitation, the tension between the high-minded neutrality of the Parisian style and the sectarian pressure groups can be observed after the 1560s, in a number of cities.

The consuls of Nîmes eventually brought in a distinguished Protestant intellectual, Jean de Serres, to direct their city's college, which was open to students of both religions. The classic Parisian style, which Touffan had defended against the Calvinist majority's encroachments, was now to be equipped with safeguards against the dangerous ideas of the pagan authors. The break with the freer practices of the past was not so sharp as to be immediately visible, but the changes introduced under de Serres' leadership are revealing.

The curriculum still required the study of Cicero, of Terence, Caesar, Virgil, and Ovid. Greek was taught beginning in the Third Form, and advanced students would eventually be able to read Plato and Plutarch in the original. What, then, has changed? On closer examination, the ministers' efforts to establish controls over the teaching and to redirect the school's goals to the study of theology, these efforts which Touffan had rebuffed, were now successful. Certain practices were abolished and censorship was introduced. "Obscene words" were to be suppressed in the pagan texts, as were all descriptions of "undesirable actions." This last requirement, especially, would surely have the effect of reducing Greek and Roman literature to a narrow trickle of doctored exemplary tales. Where such suppressions were simply not feasible, the Board of Trustees would settle for an obligatory commentary "to lessen the shock of the obscenity." In practice, then, students would end up reading carefully edited anthologies.

When the time came, in the advanced classes, to teach philosophy, instructors would be cautioned to "avoid all new ideas" and to teach "Plato and Aristotle only," settling comfortably into the Aristotelian universe which Ramus and others like him had tried so hard to explode. In fields such as political theory, mathematics, and physics, "there is to be no departure from the teaching of the Ancients." Compared to the galvanizing experience of students in the 1530s or 1540s in colleges such as Ramus's school in Paris or the Bordeaux college when Montaigne was a student, the new model college, half a century later, shaped by the needs of bishops and pastors, had become a stifling factory for indoctrination.

Instead of recommending a thorough grounding in the *optimi auctores*, as Touffan had, the rigid Board of Trustees in Nîmes now warned against the dangers of pagan literature, recommending that "those who aspire to more considerable studies" (theology, that is), should not spend "too much time enjoying the humanities." Enjoyment, as a matter of policy, was to be removed from the student experience, following the Genevan model. There were to be absolutely no theatrical performances in the college at Nîmes. Much of the pleasure and excitement which had been the hallmark of the experimental colleges in earlier years was gone now to make way for an institutional life which came close to being that of an earnest and lifeless seminary. The Trustees in Nîmes went so far as to post informers (*observatores*) in various neighborhoods of the city to report on any "indiscretions" students might be inclined to commit when they were not in class.[11]

This Calvinist adaptation of the Parisian style resembled that of the Jesuits in most ways. The Jesuits had taken over the *modus parisiensis* from the start of their experimentation with school curricula, as early as 1548.[12] At the very moment when master Touffan was confronted, in Nîmes, by the conflicting demands of the Catholic diocese and the Calvinist consistory, the old Cardinal de Tournon, now Dean of the College of Cardinals in Rome and Inquisitor General for the Kingdom of France, as well as archbishop of Lyon, opted to rely on the Jesuits, who had just come to his attention, to serve as the shock troops of the Counter-Reformation in France.

In his prime, Tournon had been a discriminating patron of Renaissance culture. Now, in 1561, the Cardinal was 72 years old and beset, from every side, by the progress of militant Protestant factions. Nowhere did the enemy, as the old Cardinal saw, make more spectacular and far-reaching conquests than in the colleges which had been founded in so many cities. The Cardinal had himself endorsed the creation of such a college in his own town of Tournon a generation earlier. At this moment, he was getting reports of heresy running wild in that college. As for the college in Lyon, under Aneau's direction it had become a haven for secret Protestant sympathizers. The city of Lyon itself, the second wealthiest in the kingdom, was almost taken over by the Protestants.

The climate of opinion in France was turning toward accommodation and compromise with the Protestant minority. Tournon was playing a key rôle in the negotiations sponsored by the Queen, Catherine de Medici, in the summer of 1561, which brought together high-level representatives of both parties. Tournon worked hard and successfully at scuttling the negotiations.

As the chief prelate in France and as the beneficiary of a vast collection of clerical incomes, he probably had more to lose than any other person should France take the English path and break with Rome. Tournon was all for using force to avoid such an outcome.[13]

Force alone could not be depended on, however. This was a war of conflicting ideologies. Tournon understood that the colleges shaped the minds of all those destined for political power. The war had to be won in the classroom. If radical masters, armed with superior learning, with their beards flying and their reckless disregard for authority, were allowed to corrupt the young, there was no way to stem the tide. Was it possible to eliminate these dangerous ideologues? In Lyon Aneau was murdered. Other principals elsewhere had been hauled before inquisitors. One could intimidate some of those secular teachers, but the urban élites were enamored with them, addicted to classical educations for their sons. One could not simply close down these colleges, which were the pride of the bourgeoisie. Would it be possible to replace secular teachers with priests? Hardly. Every such attempt faltered because of the incompetence of clerical teachers, who lacked both the expertise of the masters of the Parisian style and the confidence of the bourgeois.

At last, with the arrival of the first Jesuits, a new kind of teaching professional joined the battle against heresy. The Jesuits offered to retain the Parisian style, to provide teachers as competent as their secular counterparts, and, at the same time, to guarantee an atmosphere free of heresy.

Although their competence (*suffisance*) was usually taken for granted, rightly or wrongly, there was fierce resistance to the Jesuit bid to take over French colleges. They were viewed, with good reason, by many bourgeois families as fanatical agents of Rome and Madrid and as dangerous interlopers in the ideological wars that racked French urban society. Established interest groups, the University of Paris among them, went to court to stop the Jesuits from opening schools. As it happens, Etienne Pasquier took the case for the university, *pro bono*, early on in his career as a lawyer, a move not calculated to endear him to the Society of Jesus, whose members tended to have long memories. The struggle for control of the schools achieved epic proportions at various times. The Jesuits, implicated in accusations of regicide and conspiracy, were banished from the kingdom more than once. On the other hand, when the smoke of battle began to clear in the 1620s, as Richelieu achieved power, the French Church became an irresistible force in national affairs, and its counsel was frequently followed. Closing down as many colleges as possible, eliminating these schools of impertinence, became an objective of the government in Paris.

The effectiveness of such a campaign was modest. On the positive side, a good number of colleges located in strategic cities and provided with adequate endowments were turned over to the Society, sometimes after drawn-out battles which polarized the bourgeois. The city of Troyes, in Champagne, known for many years as the proud owner of a first-rate municipal college, resisted the Jesuit onslaught for so many years that the battle over the school occasioned a satirical volume entitled *The Siege of Troyes*.[14] In some cases, rear-guard skirmishes kept the Jesuits out for a hundred years or longer, as in the case of the city of Laon, which gave in, exhausted, only in 1723, when the Jesuits arrived, bearing royal *lettres de cachet*.[15]

The triumph of Cardinal de Tournon's policy was never complete. Even when they were being most effective, after their return from yet another exile in the 1620s, the Jesuits controlled only a portion of the dense network of classical colleges in France, and those they controlled imperfectly, since the city councils remained the owners and the Jesuits were technically their employees. Beyond their grasp lay innumerable schools in smaller towns which they chose not to contest. Even in prime locations, such as Bordeaux, they could not always dislodge the secular college and had to remain content, at times, with establishing a rival institution in town.[16] There was another handicap, which was to paralyze the best efforts of the Jesuits, of the Oratorians, of the Pères de la Doctrine Chrétienne, and of other religious orders which had been mobilized specifically to counter the danger of heresy in the schools: and that was the Parisian style itself, which they had contracted to keep alive after the departure of their bearded and independent-minded rivals.

They had no choice in the matter. City councils, even those inclined to favor the Jesuits, would agree to hire them only on the condition that they teach the very same *optimi auctores* that had been the mainstay of the curriculum for a century. Could one imagine an alternative to Plato and Cicero? How could one get on in the world without Latin and a little Greek as well? Interpret the ancients any way you like, edit out obscenities, gloss over the most perplexing passages concerning the more remarkable ideas of the pagan philosophers, surround the boys with informers and intimidate them from morning to night—even so, a classical education spelled trouble. Clever boys like Gassendi or Descartes saw right through the shabby pieties of their masters and learned to think for themselves. But even ordinary beneficiaries of their teaching could not help but notice the disparity between the mental universe of men like Garasse and that of Horace or Lucretius. The borrowed culture of the pagans was a counter-culture, permanently embedded in the Christian world, as powerful an irritant as has been, in our century, the teaching of Marxism in non-Western cultures, and with similar results.

8

Ex Tenebras Lux

THE PARTIAL VICTORY of the Counter-Reformation in France was to lead to the elimination of the Protestant minority. It also served to drive other forms of dissent underground. Yet, in spite of some school closings and in spite of the introduction of new forms of censorship, the essential traits of the *philosophe, stile de Paris*, turned out to be indelible. The daring talk that had commonly been heard in Paris, Bordeaux, or Lyon in the 1550s was eventually silenced by threats and unctuous forms of intimidation: all the same, the war against ignorance continued to be waged.

It could be that the arrest and trial of the poet Théophile de Viau in 1623 was a watershed event in the campaign against the so-called *libertins*, as Fréderic Lachèvre contended. Lachèvre, a twentieth-century supporter of Father Garasse, thought that "the happy consequence" of Garasse's campaign of intimidation was to "put off the triumph of *libertinage* for another 150 years.[1] It is worth noting that in Lachèvre's usage *libertinage* has come to mean everything associated with the eighteenth-century philosophical movement and its execrated consequence, the ideology of the French Revolution. Lachèvre was profoundly immersed in the documentary sources of seventeenth-century radicalism. He was not using the word *libertinage* loosely. He understood that words such as *libertins* or *beaux-esprits*, staples of Garasse's arsenal of invectives, were loose constructions designed to catch all varieties of resisters in the net held up for this purpose.

The events which led to Théophile de Viau's arrest were carefully planned. The young poet had been a student at the Jesuit college of La Fléche, where he had been a particular favorite of Father Voisin. Now, in the summer of 1623, while Théophile was in jail awaiting trial, Father Voisin was training novices in his care to become informers and spies ready to denounce suspect intellectuals—or *beaux-esprits*, in Garasse's ironic phrase. While Garasse was moving heaven and earth to have Théophile prosecuted and Voisin was training informers, a third Father, Guérin, kept up a barrage of maledictions in his

Sunday sermons against those who dared defend the imprisoned poet—and a shower of benedictions destined for Théophile's accusers. At the trial, things went wrong when it became clear that the principal witness for the prosecution was one of Voisin's paid informers. The poet was saved from execution, while Voisin was advised to leave the country at once.[2]

The attack against Théophile de Viau may have been inconclusive, but it signaled the starting point for a new dispensation which came into being in the aftermath of the Jesuits' return to France, after 1618. The Protestants were in retreat. The influence of the militant Catholic party and of its hardcore *dévôt* wing had not been so strong since the days of the Holy League. One consequence of this turn of events was that entire colleges were turned upside down, their teachers dispersed and replaced by members of religious congregations. It was not a comfortable time for would-be *philosophes*. There were informers everywhere. Soon the secret Company of the Holy Sacrament was to cover the entire kingdom with a network of amateur spies reporting to Jesuit fathers and denouncing criminal thoughts in perfect anonymity. Censorship in the book trade now began extending to illustrations. Fig leaves flourished, covering the shame of ancient nymphs.[3] Bigotry and false devotion were in danger of becoming fashionable to the point where one is tempted to speak of a new age dawning, the Age of Tartuffe.

The Age of Tartuffe, however, was also the age of the *honnête homme*, a designation as resonant with a variety of meanings as that of *libertin*. The extent to which the *honnête homme* gradually replaced the *libertin* is a measure of the retreat of the *dévôt* mentality, which had been triumphant in the 1620s and which was put on the defensive in the 1660s. Garasse was able to depict his enemies as secret deists or even atheists who conspired to ridicule Christian beliefs. Molière would reverse the picture. His decent characters are *honnêtes hommes*, classically educated *gens de bien*, to whom religious zeal is an embarrassment, and whose morality is that of the pagan authors. Reasonable, courteous, tolerant and well-intentioned toward others, one pictures them holding Montaigne's *Essais* or Charron's *Sagesse* in their hands. In sharp contrast with these enlightened gentlemen are scoundrels like Tartuffe, who use the appearance of religious devotion to hide their criminal desires. As for the rest of Molière's casts, they are made up mostly of fools who belong to the *sotte multitude*. Lacking a proper education—sans *science*, sans *lumières*—they cannot resist the lure of gold (Harpagon) or of empty honors (Monsieur Jourdain). Their attachment to the Church owes nothing to true piety: it is the result of fear and superstition only (Sganarelle in *Don Juan*).

The *dévôt* party, their feathers ruffled by *Tartuffe*, still had enough influence at Court to cause Louis XIV to agree, reluctantly, to forbid the play's performance in its original version, but the murderous tactics once used to frighten independent writers were blunted. The Renaissance *philosophe*, renamed *libertin* in the heat of battle, was now an *honnête homme*, liberated from the stigma of religious deviance in all but the most *dévôt* of minds.

Tartuffe, the demonic confidence man who masquerades as a saint and sets out to appropriate all of his victim's earthly possessions, meets his match in Cléante, the *honnête homme*. Cléante is the brother-in-law of Tartuffe's victim, the credulous Orgon, and he does his best to open Orgon's eyes. In vain. Orgon is incapable of seeing reason. From his point of view, Cléante is a *libertin*.

"You're talking like an atheist," Orgon warns his brother-in-law. Stung by Cléante's reasonableness, Orgon resorts to the kind of heavy-handed sarcasm which carries echoes of Garasse's attacks against the *beaux-esprits* of an earlier generation.

> "Oh, yes, you are a learned sage, I know;
> The sapience of the world within you lies;
> You alone are enlightened, truly wise,
> An oracle, a Cato, through and through;
> All other men are fools compared to you."

To which Cléante replies, as Ramus, Tahureau, or Cicero might have:

> "My only knowledge and my only art
> Is this: to tell the true and false apart."[4]

Molière's Cléante is no more of a freethinker than Pasquier had been. There may not have been anything like a *libertin* or atheist conspiracy afoot, except in the heated imagination of real-life Tartuffes,[5] but there did exist a community of shared beliefs whose origins can be traced to the classroom and which did worry cardinals and ministers of state who had learned to fear the aspirations of educated laymen, especially those who came from the lower ranks of French society. The French clergy's point of view was that there were far too many colleges "even in the smallest towns of the kingdom, to the great detriment of the State, since, by such means, merchants and even peasants find ways of getting their children to abandon trade and farming." In the same spirit, a pamphlet of the 1620s insisted on the catastrophic consequences of this "ease of access," this "bewildering number of colleges that has enabled the meanest artisans to send their children to these schools where they are taught free of charge—and this is what has ruined everything."[6]

The question of what is being ruined is left to the reader's imagination, but there was no doubt in anyone's mind about what was at stake. Writing from the opposite point of view, Gabriel Naudé, a *philosophe*, explained that "the excessive number of colleges . . . together with the ease with which books can be printed and distributed, this is what has shaken the foundations of the sects and of religion."[7]

Cardinal Richelieu was convinced that this was indeed the case. He was prepared to shut down all but a dozen of the country's colleges—and those to be staffed by reliable Jesuits—but this ambitious plan could never be set in motion.[8] Government officials kept insisting that education should be restricted: "one should teach reading, writing and counting only. Writing should not be taught to those whom Providence caused to be born peasants: such children should only learn to read."[9] However much governors and bishops may have wished France to be more like the Turkish empire, in which dissent was said to be kept at bay by controlling literacy, French cities rarely departed from their commitment to public education. They continued to cherish their colleges.

Only exceptionally can one encounter local officials currying favor by decrying the ambitious programs of rival towns and by offering to lower expectations in their own college. A memorandum from the small town of Pontoise was written in this spirit. "The teaching here differs on an essential point from the teaching of other colleges," claim the officials of Pontoise. Other colleges introduce students to higher learning (*sciences*), "thus deflecting the children from useful skills." Here, in Pontoise, on the other hand, we teach "religion, reading, writing and arithmetic" while fostering "that spirit of religion and hard-working honesty that is the mark of the citizen useful to the state," as opposed to "that spirit of idleness, arrogance and irreligion that is so costly to society."[10]

As part of the crusade against "arrogance and irreligion," the book trade, too, came under attack. It was not possible to replace the *auctores*. The best that could be achieved was to limit the circulation of their modern interpreters, the spiritual relatives of Horace, the philosopher-poet whose advice—*sapere aude!*—never ceased to inflame the passions of his modern disciples, from Ramus to Gassendi and Kant.[11] The French State gradually became more effective in its rôle as censor of subversive literature, while the Roman Index of Forbidden Books swelled in time to include just about every book that mattered, but it is hard to say whether these prophylactic measures really worked.

Montaigne's *Essais* and Pasquier's *Recherches*, for instance, did suffer an éclipse of sorts. The *Essais* had been reprinted with astonishing frequency every two years or so, from 1595 to 1669, after which year they would not be reprinted again before 1724. The book was placed on the Index in 1676. Whether this diminished its popularity is doubtful. Every ambitious theologian wrote against Montaigne, every thoughtful intellectual carried on intense imaginary conversations with him. Montaigne's book, it was said, could be found, almost invariably, in the possession of all but the most rustic of country gentlemen.

The special place Montaigne occupied was as the indispensable translator of the wisdom of the *auctores* for a broader audience. The *Essais* became the "*bréviaire des honnêtes gens*," the handbook of the *honnête homme* and *femme*. Even those readers who had no Latin could browse profitably in this encyclopedic guidebook to the authors of the Parisian style. Most of the chapters are short and all contain familiar extracts from the *auctores*, who are cited as guarantors of the author's opinions. As "the indispensable handbook for the Court and for the world," the *Essais* continued to exert a profound influence on the most diverse readers, from fashionable intellectuals such as Madame de Sévigné to obscure country priests isolated in their villages.[12] In this way the rationalism and the lively questioning of authority and tradition that was so characteristic of the college teachers of Montaigne's time lived on, illuminating the oddest corners of French life with the "*lumière de logique*."

The relatively unencumbered circulation of books made up for the greater control exercised over the colleges. Even when Montaigne—and, soon after, Bayle—were prohibited, Horace, Cicero, and Seneca circulated freely in French translation, as did the other classical authors.[13] The entire culture was saturated with the *sententiae*, the *exempla*, the *loci communes* of the ancients whom the Counter-Reformation had failed to emasculate.

The tradition established by Ramus and his contemporaries was too deeply rooted to be dismissed or circumvented. College students continued to reject dogmatic philosophy, more or less in the way Ramus had done when he was a student. Descartes' *Discours de la méthode* is in that tradition. Writing for publication, Descartes prudently chooses to operate at a level of abstraction that obscures his intellectual affinities, but Gassendi, whose *Dissertations against the Aristotelians* (1624) remained in manuscript, openly acknowledges his debt to Ramus and Charron.[14] Gassendi was a young philosophy teacher and college principal before he came to Paris and joined the radical circle around François Luillier, which included Théophile de Viau and eventually, Molière, Cyrano de Bergerac, and Gassendi's disciple, François Bernier, an adventurous physician who was to popularize Gassendi's philosophy after a long sojourn in India, which he reported on in popular travel books.[15]

Gassendi's attack against the Aristotelians was written at the very moment when the Sorbonne was persuading the *parlement* to decree the death penalty as the punishment for any aspirant to a university degree who dared to criticize Aristotle. This edict was as futile as was the obsolete form of reasoning which it sought to protect. Father Mersenne declared himself "marvelously" pleased by the severity of the prohibition, but, as Bernard Rochot points out, "serious minds no longer took scholastic philosophy seriously."[16]

Gassendi, in his *Dissertations*, makes this abundantly clear. He explains how he reached his decision to become a *philosophe* while still in school. Inoculated against the empty shell games of the theologians by his familiarity with the ancient philosophers, he took to heart Cicero's definition of true philosophy: "whoever follows its precepts will have learned to live without ever being unhappy." He realized then that there was nothing to be learned from the Aristotelians, who are "like children at the beach, building sand castles only to pull them down again."[17] With the help of his "dear Charron" and, above all, "thanks to Ramus," he learned to free himself from the debilitating mental habits acquired in childhood and to get away from the *via publica*, the *grand chemin battu* celebrated by Garasse. Fleeing the opinions of the common herd (*a gregariis opinionibus*) the true philosopher must aim for freedom, he declared, the freedom of thought (*libertas animi*) which is Nature's gift to mankind.[18]

Like Gassendi, Cyrano de Bergerac, another member of Luillier's epicurean club, cherished his *libertas animi*, refusing to believe in the reality of witchcraft "even though a number of great personages thought otherwise." This was of no consequence, since he was not prepared to defer to anyone's authority, "unless it was accompanied by Reason or came from God." Not Aristotle, not Plato, not Socrates could persuade him, "unless his own judgment was moved" by their arguments: "Reason is my queen," proclaimed Cyrano. His credo is familiar to readers of Gassendi, of Charron, of Ramus: "Let us not accept an opinion as true just because it is popular or just because a great philosopher shared it."[19]

As Olivier Bloch has pointed out, one can trace an unbroken chain of personal relations from Théophile de Viau and François Luillier's circle in the 1620s all the way to Voltaire and his correspondents in the 1720s. This connection—the materialist connection, one might call it—is only one of several paths along which the *philosophes* of the Renaissance transmitted their *libertas animi* to their eighteenth-century successors. A parallel route was that followed by Pierre Bayle, another college professor from the provinces, like Gassendi.

The son of a Protestant pastor from a small town in southwest France, Pierre Bayle studied briefly in Toulouse and converted to Catholicism only to return to his original faith within a year. As a relapsed heretic, his was a delicate position in the France of 1670. He left for Calvinist Geneva, hoping to find a teaching post there, but had to settle for private tutoring as a way of making a living. At last, in 1675, he won the competition for a chair of philosophy at the Protestant Academy in Sedan, but six years later the school was closed down by order of the government in Paris.[20]

At this point Bayle found his vocation as a writer. Beginning with his

Pensées diverses sur la comète, he embarked on a career as the most successful interpreter of sixteenth-century rationalism for the use of new generations. In Protestant Rotterdam, where he briefly occupied a chair of history and philosophy, he found himself under attack by Calvinist ministers who accused him of being a secret atheist.[21] He lost his job and turned to full-time research and writing.

Already well known for his *Pensées diverses* and for his editorship of a new journal for philosophically minded readers, the *Nouvelles de la République des Lettres*, Bayle now undertook to compose an encyclopedia, huge in scope, maddeningly intricate, and bursting with footnotes and cross-references. This *Dictionaire historique et critique* (Rotterdam, 1697, 2 vols. in fol.) was a peculiar reference work, the precursor of Diderot's *Encyclopédie*. It was a recipe book for would-be *philosophes*, teaching them subtly to doubt the eternal verities Father Mersenne had once hoped to assemble in an encyclopedia of his own. Closely attuned to the scholarship of an earlier age and instinctively critical of received ideas, Bayle pleased himself by praising the moral qualities of pagan philosophers. In his article on Democritus, in which he relies on Lambin and Montaigne, Bayle admits that this admirable philosopher had no use for the gods. "This particular error," comments Bayle, "is never made by small minds. Only great minds are capable of it."[22]

That atheism was not necessarily an invitation to vice is a constant theme in Bayle's writings, as, indeed, it had been in the writings of earlier *philosophes*. How could it be otherwise, raised as they were to admire Greek philosphers and Roman heroes? When they lifted their eyes from the pages of their dear *auctores*, who preached reason and tolerance, they saw nothing but the catastrophic consequences of religious fanaticism. "We have the hearts of executioners," lamented Descaurres, the college principal from Amiens, while reminding his readers that all the pagan philosophers agreed that "to subject a man to torture is a cruel and inhumane practice."[23] A century later, Bayle pointed out, with evident relish, that "it is no more surprising to see an atheist living virtuously than it is to see a Christian committing all sorts of crimes."[24] Is it possible, asks Bayle, "to conceive of *honnêteté*," without believing that there is a God?[25] His answer is, of course, in the affirmative. *Honnêteté* had come to mean, in the vocabulary of seventeenth-century philosophical writers, the natural virtue of rational individuals—pagan, Christian, Brazilian, or Chinese. This rare and essential quality they understood to be independent of any religious teaching.

Not surprisingly, Bayle's *Pensées diverses*, like Montaigne's *Essais*, could serve as a breviary for *philosophes*. The marquis d'Argens, in his memoirs, tells of an occasion when he was at sea, caught in a sudden storm between Rome and Livorno. "The sailors called on all the Virgins of Italy, a monk said his prayers while crying piteously, two Calvinists recited Marot's psalms, while I stood on deck, reading Bayle's *Pensées diverses* to take my mind off the crisis. The other passengers, seeing me read my book so calmly, thought I must be a Saint, at peace with himself because of his tranquil conscience."[26]

Bayle's *Pensées diverses* hardly contain new ideas. It was not originality that was prized in such works. On the contrary, each contributor to the corpus of anti-scholastic writings, from Ramus to Bayle, repeated much the same commonplaces culled from the *auctores* and each of them recounted suspiciously similar dramas of *déniaisement* and *liberté philosophique*.[27] The marquis d'Argens, reading Bayle on the deck of his sinking ship, surrounded by panic-stricken monks and sailors, reminds the reader of Erasmus' colloquy, *The Shipwreck*. As for the stories about adolescents who flee the *ténèbres* of their Aristotelian mentors to wander into bookshops where they discover Euclid's *Elements*, or a similar instrument of enlightenment, they are so common that one might as well stop counting them.

Fontenelle, the philosophical man of letters *par excellence*, who knew everyone, speaking of a friend of his, reports that "one day, when he was studying philosophy with the Jesuits in Caen, he chanced upon Euclid in a bookstore. All at once, the eternal uncertainty, the sophistical awkwardness, the pointless obscurity . . . of the philosophy of the schools were contrasted with the lucidity, the coherence, the certainty of the truths of geometry." The same Fontenelle, speaking of the theologian Malebranche, tells us that "one day, as he was walking along the rue St. Jacques, a bookseller drew his attention to the *Traité de l'Homme* by Monsieur Descartes, which had just been published. Malebranche was 26 years old at the time. He was struck as if by light (*frappé comme d'une lumière*). Scholastic philosophy had not seemed to him to be a philosophy at all."

Another candidate for enlightenment, according to Fontenelle, "lost his taste for what was being taught in the philosophy classes. There was nothing in all this which had anything to do with Nature, but only vague and abstract ideas which missed their targets, so to speak, without ever touching them."

According to Fontenelle, Malebranche's own writings eventually triggered the same kind of instant illumination in the mind of young Louis Carré, who "was suddenly transported from the dark (*ténèbreuse*) scholastic philosophy to the source of a luminous and brilliant philosophy. All at once, all things were new to him again, and a new universe was unveiled before his eyes." Speaking of his own experience with the logicians, Fontenelle reports that he "soon saw that there was no need to understand what they were saying, that these were only words,"[28] which is very much the conclusion Gassendi had reached when he decided that his teachers were building sand castles only to tear them down.

Linked to each other by the inevitable reading list of their college years, the writers who spoke for the *honnêtes hommes* expressed themselves with remarkable unanimity. Their teachers tried to steer them away from dangerous thoughts,[29] but even among Jesuit fathers the determination to thwart independent thinking could be seen weakening. Fontenelle was on good terms with men like Father Buffier, S.J., who had been a classmate of his at the college in Rouen. Buffier's ideas, it seems, were pretty close to his own.[30] Another Rouen Jesuit, Father David, was an admirer of Gassendi's epicurean philosophy.[31] Pierre Bayle, who was staying in Rouen in 1674, testifies to the open-mindedness of the local intellectual élite whose members met every Thursday in the home of the magistrate and Greek scholar Etienne Bigot. Bigot was a Catholic, but in Pasquier's manner, "not ill-intentioned toward us," reports Bayle, who notes that pastors and abbés got along perfectly well on those occasions.[32]

In Paris, Fontenelle frequented the salon of Madame de la Sablière, a Gassendist circle where one could encounter Dr. Bernier as well as the poet La Fontaine. This was only one of a number of salons "in which those who had a genuine interest in true learning assembled in little bands, like rebels conspiring against ignorance and the dominant prejudices."[33] Another rallying point was the circle around the abbé Bourdelot, whose motto proclaimed: "we go straight for the truth and no authority means anything to us."[34]

Whether they had been raised as Catholics or as Protestants, whether their philosophical radicalism diverged only modestly from accepted norms or whether it went beyond that, the journalists, poets, mathematicians, and *curieux* in general had all attended good colleges, all read the same books. They were all open to the same influences. In and out of the Parisian salons, familiar with publishers and booksellers, they all spoke the same language. Any one of them could have dropped into an ongoing debate about physics, geometry, biblical scholarship, or Roman history, and joined in without missing a beat. The enlightened few, always appropriately contemptuous of the *sotte multitude*—("*Le critère du pire, c'est la foule,*" confides Fontenelle[35])—seem to have been, throughout, urban, bourgeois, and male.

That women writers should have been few in number is hardly surprising, since girls were not admitted to colleges before the twentieth century. Tutored at home, a number of remarkable women played a part in the *philosophes'* ascent anyway. There was Montaigne's chosen literary executor and adopted daughter, Mademoiselle de Gournay, whose salon in the 1620s served as an occasional rallying point for free spirits implicated in Théophile de Viau's trial.[36] Even in the early days, when Baïf, Ronsard, Du Bellay, and Pasquier were young, there were feminine presences lurking in the wings, known not only for their charm but for their learning.[37] From Mademoiselle de Gournay to Madame Du Deffand, there were women who wrote and whose opinions counted—but, then, they too belonged to the fashionable circles, Parisian for the most part, which Fontenelle, among other chroniclers of the intelligentsia, recorded for posterity.

The real mystery remains: how far did the ideas of the *philosophes* travel? Did they reach beyond city limits? Could they penetrate the lower reaches of French society? And if so, by what means? The attentive reader may not need to be reminded that among the earliest scatterings of adventurous minds, there were men like Ramus, who came from the bottom of the heap, as the orphaned son of a charcoal-burner, even if, in later life, he invented an implausible aristocratic ancestry for himself, this being the habitual method for regularizing the status of successful people of improbably squalid origins.[38] Other examples from the early sixteenth century come to mind, including that of Pierre Belon. It is true that this was in a period of rapid social mobility, when the son of an itinerant peddler could rise to wealth and a judgeship.[39] Later, in the course of the seventeenth century, when every effort was made to deny access to *sciences*, and even to basic literacy, to those whom Providence had caused to be born the children of simple peasants, it may have been more difficult for gifted farmers' sons to rise in the world.

On the other hand, just as the imposition of censorship in the book trade and of clerical control over urban colleges failed to achieve foolproof results, so the official policy of preserving ignorance at the village level may have been less than completely successful. As long as there were village schools and itinerant teachers—the bearded kind, free of clerical ties—the effects of what Lachèvre called *libertinage* would be felt. There was hardly a village in France that did not hire at least one schoolteacher in the off-season. Such a teacher might take on both boys and girls, over the bishop's protests. Sometimes he brought his wife along to teach the girls. It was the village community that chose to hire teachers and to pay their wages. At times, diocesan authorities objected to the village's choice of candidates for the teaching post, but the matter was mostly out of the Church's hands.[40]

What did such teachers bring to the village? Mostly, one has to assume, they taught what they were hired to teach: reading, writing, and arithmetic. The families that paid their wages and provided the small room in which classes were held had specific and limited goals in mind. They wanted their children to acquire the basic skills that might propel them from the farm to more rewarding prospects in town. The village élite of *laboureurs*, that handful of farmers who owned enough land to prosper, or at least to avoid crushing debt and eventual destitution, considered a basic education indispensable. Their children would become *laboureurs-marchands*, handling contracts and standing up to the money lenders and cattle dealers. Eventually, one of their children or grand-children might abandon farm work altogether, marrying a bourgeois or becoming a priest.[41]

The presence of schoolteachers in the villages was not without risk, from the Church's point of view. The occasional teacher might well be a reader of books. He might know Latin. He might be a reader of Montaigne. He might be a secret heretic or atheist. From the point of view of bishops who prized obedience above all, ignorance was a quality to be cultivated in peasants, and all opportunities for connections to the larger world beyond had best be avoided. To ignore such precautions was dangerous, as we shall discover from the cautionary tale of a peasant boy named Jean Meslier. The son of a *laboureur-marchand* in the village of Mazerny, Jean was born in 1664. Mazerny was a small and poor village consisting of no more than 68 households. Situated in a generally luckless region ravaged by passing troops, Mazerny was only a short ride away from the city of Sedan, a Protestant stronghold until the expulsion of 1685. Poor though it was, the village maintained a schoolteacher. He was a married man, Jean Mairy, whose links to the Meslier family were close enough so that Jean Meslier, when he was fourteen, acted as godfather to the Mairys' newborn son.

By then, Jean probably had learned all that master Mairy could teach him. He was admitted to a seminary in Reims and, at the age of 25, in 1689, he was appointed *curé* of the village of Etrepigny, which was half the size of Mazerny, probably even more miserable, but only a day's walk from his parents' home. There he stayed, fulfilling his duties, until his death, in 1729. In the course of those forty years, he seems to have hardly ever left his village. His entire existence would have been unremarkable, and we would know no more about him than we know about thousands of other country priests, except for one thing: at some point in his life, sensing the approach of death, he began composing a lengthy memoir, a record of his innermost thoughts.

A prudent man, Meslier made sure that no one could guess what he was really thinking. He had no taste for martyrdom. But on paper, speaking to posterity, Meslier held nothing back. He made two copies of his memoir and hid them in such a way that they were bound to be discovered after his death. Once discovered, the secret thoughts of the *curé* of Etrepigny joined the stream of clandestine tracts, the *samizdat* of the Old Régime, which ferried suspect literature to the libraries of well-to-do amateurs. A copy of Meslier's memoir thus reached the desk of the most effective publicist of his time, Voltaire, who chose to abridge and edit a portion of Meslier's feverish writings and to publish this as "the testament of the *curé* Meslier."

In this version, the scandalous memoir achieved considerable success. About its author, nothing was known until recently. For all anyone knew, the country priest could have been invented by Voltaire. It was only in 1965, with the publication of Maurice Dommanget's ground-breaking and meticulous study,[42] and in 1970, with the publication of the original text of the *Mémoire des pensées et sentiments de Jean Meslier*,[43] that Meslier emerged from anonymity. A number of studies have added to our understanding of Meslier's world since then, making it possible to guess, at least in this instance, how the ideas of the *philosophes* could penetrate the deepest recesses of rural life.[44]

Meslier himself, in the opening pages of his autograph confessions, claims that he had reached his surprising conclusions at an early age, presumably when he was still a schoolboy, tutored by Jean Mairy.[45] There is no reason to doubt him. The village schoolteacher is a natural suspect as the chief instrument of the boy's *déniaisement*, but he is hardly the only one. Dommanget, and others in his wake, have demonstrated that the entire region between Mazerny and Sedan was a hotbed of heterodoxy, disobedience, and underground rancor. There were considerable numbers of Protestants, not only in the city of Sedan, but in the countryside, before the expulsions of 1685. A village close to Mazerny still had a Protestant pastor in 1678, when Jean was finishing his studies with Mairy. This pastor, Pierre Béguin, according to one source, was a secret atheist.[46] The local *seigneur*, in Etrepigny, had been a Protestant. His widow still lived there when the young *curé* Meslier arrived to take charge of his decrepit church, a twelfth-century building with a leaking roof and empty of even the barest furnishings.

From his observation post in Etrepigny, Meslier could not help hearing of the devastation caused by the king's policies. Protestants, deprived of all rights, were hounded to death, while soldiers, both French and foreign, sacked villages along their passage. Of Mazerny's 60 houses, 28 were in ruins. In Reims, where Meslier had been a seminarian, half the population was reduced to begging.[47] There seems to have been little respect for the government or for the Church among Meslier's parishioners, many of whom could be found at the local tavern during Sunday morning church services. In addition to the presence of secret Protestants, rumors pointed to the presence of atheists, and reports reached the bishop that spoke of teenagers getting together at parties (*veillées*) on winter nights, at which they mocked the mass.[48]

This was a wretched world Meslier was contemplating, a world in which the mass of the population, *le pauvre peuple*, was perpetually mistreated by the *grands*, the lords who controlled everything: land, government and Church. Not that this state of affairs was exceptional in the France of Louis XIV, but Meslier took the sufferings of his *chers amis* to heart with the fierce passion of an Old Testament prophet. He entrusted his *pensées* only to his secret notebook, knowing perfectly well what would happen to him "had he told anyone what he really thought."[49] Once dead, however, he would be beyond the reach of the authorities. Having unmasked, in his *mémoire*, the comspiracies which robbed human beings of their natural rights, he had done something hardly anyone had dared to do before him as far as he knew. There were other enlightened and honest observers, but they chose not to speak out, fearing for their lives. Shrewdly, Meslier planned his exploit, year after year, filling his notebook with bitter thoughts, and expecting his call to revolution to reach the world after his death. He had no children, he had no possessions, he had traveled light while alive. After his death, when his secret thoughts were bound to cause a scandal, "let them call me whatever they like: impious, apostate, atheist. This will not bother me in the least. They may do what they wish with my body. Let them tear it to pieces, hack it into bits, roast it, fricassé it, eat it, cover it with sauces: I will be beyond their reach entirely, I will no longer have anything to fear."[50]

Speaking from the grave, Meslier confesses to his *"chers amis"* that he led a double life ever since he was a boy. He never believed that religion was anything but a masquerade. He became a priest to please his parents. For forty years he found himself keeping up the pretense, performing rituals which he knew to be meaningless. For this he apologizes. He failed to speak up and tell the truth while he lived for fear of persecution. Now he is ready to make up for his silence.

He begins his revelations by reminding his dear friends of what they already know but cannot explain, namely that the world they live in is a terrible place.[51] A terrible place, that is, for all but the privileged few, the *riches* and the *grands* [8]. Those *beaux messieurs*, kept in ease and luxury by the sweat and blood of the mass of the people, know how to deflect their victims' complaints by urging them to address futile prayers to gods and saints who cannot hear them [22].

The cause of all the injustice and unhappiness in the world is the complicity of priests with tyrants [10]. Taking advantage of the ignorance and credulity of the weakest and least enlightened among men, the priests make them believe whatever they like and pounce upon their worldly goods like greedy wolves [12], on the pretext of leading them to experience eternal bliss in a heaven of their invention [13].

All religions are false [39]. They were invented by shrewd politicians with the complicity of priests. This sinister alliance is the source of all the injustice in the world [10]. For Nature, originally, created all men equal and intended them to live in harmony.[52] The rapacious lords and their hypocritical accomplices, the priests, have perverted Nature's order for their own benefit.

That the poor, ignorant masses who lack *science* should fail to see through this plot is not surprising, but what Meslier could not understand at first was the silence of those who are educated and who understand the hidden mechanism of this age-old conspiracy. Eventually, he reached the conclusion that those enlightened bystanders choose to conform, at least outwardly, as he himself had done, because they do not want to risk their lives and possessions—and the welfare of their families—by opposing the errors of the multitude and by resisting the authority of tyrants. It is not fear alone that keeps enlightened observers from denouncing the practices of tyrants. Like La Boëtie before him, Meslier sees the privileged classes as clients of tyrants, linked to them, as if by a rope, by means of the benefits they derive from their patronage.[53]

What is to be done? Has not the time come, at last, when the "*pauvres peuples*" will be delivered from their "miserable slavery"? When "the rich and the great of this world" will stop looting and oppressing them? And stop abusing them "with all kinds of idolatries and superstitions [34]?" It is up to the enlightened (*éclairés*) to accomplish this task. Only *gens d'esprit* can disabuse the *peuples* of their errors and show them how odious is the excessive authority of the *grands;* they must encourage the people to throw off the tyrant's yoke. They must teach them these fundamental truths: that they should follow the *lumières* of human reason alone and abide by the laws of natural equity, probity and justice, without the interference of imposters, idolators, and superstitious godlings (*deicoles*).[54]

If it comes to that, confides Meslier in what, for him, is a humorous aside, we may have to strangle all the *grands* with the intestines of priests, a suggestion made in his hearing by a man of his acquaintance who lacked a formal education but who had plenty of common sense. What the man said "may strike some as crude and shocking," comments Meslier, but one has to admit that this is what those kinds of people—the lords and the priests—truly deserve. He would liquidate these monsters himself, if he could, Meslier confesses, "not for revenge, not out of hatred," but only becuase of his love of justice and truth.[55]

Stripped of such occasional outbursts, Meslier's call for liberation and for a return to the natural freedom and equality of the Golden Age is entirely in keeping with a long tradition of academic discussion. In his conclusion, he calls for a general uprising of the oppressed in terms that are very close to those La Boëtie had used: your salvation lies in your own hands, he tells his *chers amis*; the power of tyrants proceeds from the timidity of their subjects; unite, if you are wise, if you have enough courage; communicate with each other, write down what you think, the way I did, and expose the errors and superstitions that make slaves of you.[56]

When Meslier's "Testament" surfaced, in Voltaire's shrewdly edited version, it was read as an astonishing and unique document which proved that a simple country priest could reach enlightened conclusions all on his own. Since the 1960s, with the publication of the full text of the *Mémoire* and with the scrutiny that it has received, it is becoming clearer that Meslier, in spite of his isolation, was able to hitch on to a tradition that extended from the Stoic and Epicurean philosophers to Montaigne, Charron, and Naudé, among *philosophes* closer to his own time. Like a tramp riding the rails, Meslier jumped onto anything within his reach, grabbing an admonition from Ecclesiastes or from the Gospels (*vous êtes tous frères*),[57] assuming an honorary membership in "*le parti de la vérité*,"[58] using Montaigne's handy description of manipulation (*brides à veaux*, ropes for pulling calves along),[59] and always lighting, as surely as a laser beam, onto the most provocative citations from the *auctores*.[60]

As it happens, then, this particular village *curé* was able to tap into the high culture of the Parisian style from his obscure parsonage where he led a quiet existence enlivened only by his dear forbidden Montaigne and by a succession of equally forbidden young female "cousins" in his household, whom he refused to part with, in spite of the bishop's protests.[61]

What if Jean Meslier had not been as serious a seeker after truth, what if he had chosen to avoid prohibited books, what if he had been a simpler and less tenacious man, satisfied with reading only authorized or popular books? Even then, probably, he could not have avoided stumbling across the battle cries employed in the war against ignorance.

A case in point is a book much favored and frequently cited in his *Mémoire*, a popular book entitled *L'espion dans les cours des princes chrétiens*, which first appeared in 1684, when Meslier was a young seminarian.[62] This book went through many editions. In it, a fictional Turkish spy delivers judgments on the behavior of the Christians he observes, much in the way that Montesquieu's Persians will, some years later. This particular Turk appears deeply and dangerously involved in the philosophical debates of the Parisian salons.

He is a supporter of Copernicus,[63] and he dreams of mingling with *philosophes*.[64] He is full of nostalgia for that Golden Age "when the world, still in its infancy, did not know what bigotry was and when Reason had not yet been corrupted by pious fables, . . . before superstition had begun representing divinity under barbarous and terrible forms." He himself believes "in an eternal God," allows the philosophical Turk, "but if an angel were to come down from the sky and started telling me monstrous and unbelievable things . . . I would beg him to excuse me and I would suspend my belief."[65]

In matters concerning religion, the Turkish spy is inclined to put his trust only in those beliefs that seem reasonable to him. He is struck, in his observation of believers, by the fact that "they have a hundred different sects," although it stands to reason that "there is only one truth," an observation not without precedent.[66] He notes that atheism is thriving in Christian lands and points out that the corrupt ways of the Papacy contribute mightily to this state of affairs,[67] a conclusion reached by any number of Christian writers, including Pasquier, long ago. This Turk notes, as Naudé and others had noted already, the unsettling influence of the printed book and of public education. He claims to know of ordinary peasants in Christian lands who can speak Greek and Latin and artisans who are *philosophes*.[68]

Is this Turk an atheist? He is in a quandary. He sees, in every religion, equal parts of truth and falsehood. As a result, he finds it impossible to decide in favor of one religion or another. He suspects "that all these different cults may have been invented by politicians, each of them adapting the basic model to the inclinations of the people they intended to take advantage of."[69] On balance, the Turk begins to sound like a Deist. "There are people in the West," he confides, "who are called Deists. They believe that one should embrace in one's religion only those things which are compatible with reason." These Deists, he hastens to explain, are not Atheists: "they should really be considered *philosophes*." Reaching his conclusion, the Turk explains that he would like "to equate piety with those qualities which others consider the source of Atheism."[70]

Judging from the sentiments expressed in a popular work such as *L'espion*, even the most daring views held by exiled and forbidden *philosophes* were reaching an audience of considerable size. Pierre Bayle wrote for a refined and scholarly reader. His *Dictionaire* was expensive and forbidden. *L'espion*, on the other hand, demanded little effort or preparation from the reader, even while introducing him to truly subversive notions by means of amusing fictional exchanges. An angry man like Jean Meslier, thirsting for justice, found corroboration for his own direct observations of human nature in such books. The Turkish spy keeps remarking that religion is put to unholy uses. "There is no doubt that religion makes the common people more obedient to their superiors," he observes,[71] explaining that "all religious ceremonies have a political purpose" and that "the earliest lawgivers felt free to create gods as they pleased."[72] Such observations are straight out of Montaigne.[73] Meslier would have found them doubly convincing, especially since the Turkish spy has a heart of gold and shares Meslier's boundless anger when he allows himself to contemplate the evils for which he holds the *grands* of this world, and their apologists, fully responsible. He truly hates those "masked cannibals" who devour the "marrow of the poor" and drink the "blood of widows and orphans": they imagine that they can appease Heaven by building temples and by endowing convents."[74] The Turk's expression, "masked cannibals," reminds one of La Boëtie's "*mange-peuples*" and Rabelais' "*demovores*."

The Turk has no illusions about the nobility and the source of its privileges. "The ancestors of these people who make such a fuss, were cruel and bloodthirsty oppressors and tyrants, thieves and parricides. In a word, the most ancient nobility was nothing but meanness backed by power."[75] This

Turk sounds very much like other critics of the nobility's privileges, master Descaurres, for instance, the college principal in Amiens, whose furious comments on the idleness, the vices, the murderous propensities and the sinister objectives of the nobility were recorded in his *Oeuvres morales* of 1584.[76]

Enlightened readers of *L'espion*, bent upon evading the tentacular reach of "*les bigots*," were offered the choice of living "*en philosophes*,"[77] of rejecting the claims of established churches and privileged aristocrats. They were invited to dream of a better world in which reason, virtue, and *science* alone would govern the minds of men, putting an end to intolerance and oppression. No longer confined to the classrooms which served privileged adolescents mostly, such ideas were acquiring wings, fulfilling the prophecies of those who feared the consequences of uncontrolled learning.

Generations of college teachers had extracted a coherent philosophy from the pagan classics, a philosophy which could act as a counterpoise to the fatalistic instructions contained in officially approved sermons. Instead of accepting the world as it was constituted, a world of masters and servants, of privilege and punishment, they could imagine a better world in which distinctions of rank and wealth would vanish. The task ahead was clearly spelled out. Once they were taught to read and to think for themselves, more and more converts would join the war against ignorance. They would see the *lumières* of Reason and join the *philosophes* in their campaign to restore that Golden Age when neither the ownership of property nor the conspiracies of venal priests stood in the way of man's instinctive pursuit of happiness.

These ideas were rooted in French urban society more deeply than in German lands, one suspects, and disseminated more freely in France than in those countries where schooling was more effectively controlled by ecclesiastical overseers. It was no accident that what we call the Enlightenment of the eighteenth century turned out to be, above all, a French phenomenon. If one considers the French Enlightenment, not as a period piece enlivened by amusing rhetoric, but as a political movement that transformed the destiny of those who were reached by its call to action, it stands to reason that the sources of this movement need to be understood. In these pages the author chose to privilege two creations of the Renaissance—the printed book in its vernacular guise and the public school—as the vehicles by means of which classical commonplaces were transported to new destinations.

How far they traveled can be gauged from the following passage, taken from Thomas Jefferson's famous last letter, in which the old *philosophe* calls on men "to burst the chains under which monkish ignorance and superstition had persuaded them to bind themselves." Sounding very much like La Boëtie, Ramus, or Meslier, Jefferson speaks of "the general spread of the light of science," which he believes "has already laid open to every view the palpable truth, that the mass of mankind has not been born with saddles on their backs, nor a favored few, booted and spurred, ready to ride legitimately by the grace of God."[78]

This is as elegant a summation as one could wish for of the legacy the *philosophes* of the French Renaissance passed on to their heirs.

9

The Republic of Letters

THE IMPORTANCE OF THE LEGACY of the early *philosophes* is not easy to evaluate. It is clear enough that the *philosophes* of Jefferson's youth viewed their own much advertised enlightenment as an achievement prepared, over the course of several generations, by pioneers who had struggled under difficult conditions. Peter Ramus was a case in point. He had been "a good *philosophe* in an age when it would be hard to think of more than three of them," wrote Voltaire, noting that Ramus had lived the life of a virtuous man against the grain of the "criminal epoch" into which he had been born. As a member of a beleaguered and hardy minority, Ramus could not be expected to display the sort of ease and style prized in eighteenth-century salons. Voltaire was prepared to stretch a point and grant, without much conviction, that Ramus, that embattled and disputatious professor, was also "*si l'on veut*," a "*bel esprit.*"[1] In his rôle as arbiter and guarantor of philosophical pedigrees, Voltaire was more comfortable extolling the accomplishments of someone like Pierre Bayle, whom he was prepared to recognize as "the greatest dialectitian ever." Bayle's Dictionary, wrote Voltaire, had been "the first work of this kind by means of which one could learn to think."[2]

On the whole, Voltaire's contemporaries, those who thought of themselves as *philosophes*, did look back to their predecessors with respect, a respect, in some instances, that bordered on hagiography. They subscribed to the notion that, between the living and the dead, between French or Chinese or ancient Greek rationalists, a link existed, a solidarity so passionate that "they must all think of each other as brothers," wrote Bayle in his *Nouvelles de la République des Lettres.*[3]

Was there any need to spell out the conditions of admission to this eminent brotherhood whose membership had included the likes of Democritus, Socrates, Cicero, and Horace? Did not everyone know how to recognize a *philosophe*, even if he happened to be Chinese or Iroquois, let alone if he was a Frenchman known for having objected to superstition and intolerance? Only a Prussian professor would bother to explain the obvious and provide a systematic analysis of the meaning of Enlightenment, as Immanuel Kant did in a pompous essay published in the *Berlinische Monatschrift* of December 1784, under the title of "Beantwortung der Frage: Was ist Aufklärung?"

Enlightenment, Kant explains, is that remarkable condition brought about by a person's withdrawal from dependence, from that dependence—*servitude*, in La Boëtie's vocabulary—which is the consequence of allowing others to govern our minds. In Kant's analysis, as in La Boëtie's, this slavish capitulation to received ideas is entirely self-inflicted (*selbstverschuldet*). Its cause is the fear felt by most men when it comes to thinking for themselves. This fear, to be sure, has always been shrewdly exploited by tyrants who find it easier to govern subjects when they are reduced to the unthinking obedience of domestic animals (*Hausvieh*). Kant, like La Boëtie, believes that the mighty of this world conspire to turn their subjects into dumb animals.

How, then, can one expect mankind to recapture its independence? Kant's answer resembles that given by La Boëtie. He believes that in the midst of the great herd (*grosse Haufen*) of sheep-like followers, there are always a few exceptional beings to be found who are naturally inclined to resist the common path: they know how to think for themselves, they are *Selbstdenker*.

Kant is stating the classic position of earlier *philosophes*. He cites the obvious battle cries out of the classroom (*sapere aude*) and the commonplaces, out of Cicero and Seneca, in favor of liberty of thought. Such ideas are dangerous, he recognizes. It would be premature to act upon them. The time is not at hand, he concedes, for true enlightenment. It would, in fact, be imprudent to permit anyone except a few licensed intellectuals in the State's service ("*öffentliche Gelehrte*") to speak out on such matters since, if the truth be known, there is, as yet, only one truly enlightened person in Germany: the king himself, Frederick the Great. Most of Kant's article, after the ringing declarations of the opening paragraphs, is devoted to shameless praise of his ultimate master. We are a long way from La Boëtie's principled contempt for monarchs.

Still, in spite of differences attributable to the lesser or greater exercise of ordinary prudence, among other variables, there are some fundamental beliefs shared by *philosophes*, whether they are writing about botany in 1553 or leading a new nation to independence in 1776. These beliefs, almost without exception, can be traced to the *optimi auctores*, and this goes a long way toward explaining the coherence of the philosophical movement, since the definition of an educated person barely changed at all over a period of three centuries.

Jefferson, writing from Paris to his nephew Peter in August of 1785, advises the boy to "begin a course of ancient history, reading everything in the original." Among the authors he recommends are Herodotus, Thucydides, Xenophon, Livy, Sallust, Caesar, Cicero, and Tacitus. For poetry, he recommends Horace, Euripides, and Sophocles. Moral lessons are to be sought in Epictetus, in Seneca, in Plato's dialogues, and in Cicero's philosophical works. As for science and mathematics, Uncle Thomas suggests that Peter get busy learning French, "because the books, when you advance in Mathematics, Natural Philosophy or Natural History, will be mostly in French, these sciences being better treated by the French than the English writers."[4]

Aside from the progress made since the mid-sixteenth century in science and mathematics, nothing had changed since Michel Eyquem, the future Monsieur de Montaigne, entered the public college of Bordeaux at the age of 6, in 1540. The style of Paris eventually ceased to be a novelty. One spoke, more generally, of studying the humanities—"*Il a fait ses humanités*" in such and such a college, one said—and one could be reasonably certain that the books on the reading list and the skills to be acquired would be much the same in most colleges, in sixteenth-century Gascony or eighteenth-century Virginia. Was it worth pointing out how revolutionary these humanities continued to be, how quickly and completely they had replaced the knowledge purveyed by medieval universities?

In France, the introduction of new colleges in the manner of Paris, beginning in the 1520s, had the effect of severing the connection between learning and theology. Instead of studying Latin grammar in preparation for theology courses, as they once had, students began to receive a broad introduction to Greek and Roman culture presented as an end in itself—and as the key to the pursuit of happiness.

The *optimi auctores*, some of them, had been read and appreciated, of course, before the 1520s and before they were printed. They had provided private and extracurricular pleasures to Erasmus' contemporaries. The Parisian style simply institutionalized these adventurous pursuits. No longer reserved for exceptionally gifted philologists, who taught themselves Greek like Erasmus or traveled to Italy to confer with Greek émigré scholars as Lazare de Baïf had done, the *auctores* were now available in their original languages, in hundreds of classrooms, to the children of ordinary families, in every French town. What made France different from the rest of Europe was the profusion of public, tuition-free classical day schools controlled by local elected officials and staffed by secular teachers.

Almost imperceptibly, but very quickly, the purpose of learning was redefined in France. Elsewhere, medieval universities were refitted so as to include the humanities without putting an end to the traditional function of the university, the training, that is, of priests and ministers.[5] The universities, in their moribund phase, remained practical institutions. One attended them to be certified as a Doctor of Theology or Medicine. Whatever one might think of their deficiencies, one valued their diplomas even if these could be, on occasion, simply purchased after a brief pretense of studious attendance.

The new colleges, on the other hand, were not practical at all. They did not usually issue diplomas. They prepared for no jobs, at least not obviously. They could not be described as way stations on the road to Higher Education since there was no serious expectation on anyone's part of learning anything worthwhile outside of the colleges. The study of law, of medicine, or of theology was understood to be no more than professional training as opposed to true learning.

In almost every respect, the colleges in the Parisian style had entirely supplanted the medieval university. They replaced a clerical model of occupational training with a secular model of education leading not to an occupation but to "happiness," as the college principal Pierre Gassendi explained in a letter to Pasquier's old classmate, Guy du Faur de Pibrac.[6]

Gassendi was the son of simple farmers. Born in 1592, he grew up on the outskirts of the small Provençal mountain town of Digne, in whose public school he acquired all the *bonae literae* required of an educated person. At the age of 20, he was named principal of the school in Digne. A few years later he obtained a doctorate in theology at Aix, took holy orders, and was soon launched in his career as a *philosophe* with a predilection for Epicurus. In his letter to Pibrac, in 1621, Gassendi paid his respects to that "most happy century"—*saeculum felicius*—the past century, that is, in the course of which "good letters were restored."[7]

As much a professor as Kant was to be, Gassendi tends to be systematic in describing the benefits to be expected from the study of the *auctores*, when conducted in the spirit of his admired mentors, Charron, Montaigne, and Ramus. Like Jefferson, Gassendi stresses the utility of historical studies "which clear the past of obscurity and remove confusion" and which, moreover, "provide a way for our minds to see and to understand, with the help of the past, what to expect of the future." What Gassendi hopes to achieve by means of historical investigations is the discovery of "the purpose of life" and of "the meaning of this universal comedy." The study of philosophy, in his view, was not meant to lead to a diploma or to an academic dissertation, but to the achievement of happiness. Elusive though this objective may seem, Gassendi appears to believe in the possibility of future progress when he agrees with Seneca that "the time will come when our descendants will marvel at our ignorance."[8]

It is difficult to escape the conclusion that the *saeculum felicius* which stretched from the lifetime of Erasmus to that of Gassendi proved to be the laboratory in which a specifically modern reading of the "universal comedy" was developed, and that this was done on so large a scale, especially in France, that it would be a mistake to think of the "war against ignorance" as a guerrilla war waged by a handful of *libertins*.

The notion of *libertinage* is an obstacle to clear thinking about the origins of the Enlightenment. A stereotype invented by the sworn enemies of the *philosophes*, the word *libertin* was designed to act as a semantic trap by means of which the *philosophe* became inseparable from the immoralist and the voluptuary. Was the *libertin* a cynical *roué* addicted to licentious pleasures beyond the reach of the multitudes—or was he an uncompromising rationalist like Gassendi or Spinoza?

To think of seventeenth-century rationalists as exceptional creatures with a penchant for drunken orgies is a misunderstanding even Garasse and Mersenne were unlikely to make. From the vantage point of these embattled traditionalists who wished only to obey and to believe, the *lumières* invoked by the *philosophes* threatened the souls, not of a handful of notoriously debauched eccentrics, but of entire generations of schoolboys.

At the conclusion of this study, the reader may be inclined to share this judgment. Without pronouncing on the eventual fate of endangered souls, it seems reasonable to shift the focus of inquiries into the origins of the Enlightenment from a catalogue of martyrs, of men said to be ahead of their times who were persecuted for their advocacy of unorthodox ideas, to a far broader constituency. Having graduated from colleges where they had read the standard pagan moralists and where they had been invited to consider the proofs of geometry as models for unobstructed thinking, the most conventional of men became candidates for enlightenment.

NOTES

1. Portrait of a Discreet *Philosophe*

1. On Aramon's expedition, see Charles Scheffer, ed., *Le Voyage de M. d'Aramon* (Paris, 1887). The document presented by Scheffer is an account of the voyage by Jean Chesneau, the ambassador's secretary. The editor provides a wealth of useful information concerning French travelers in the Levant.

2. On the bright young scholars and scientists in Tournon's entourage, see Henri Potez, "Deux années de le Renaissance," *Revue d'histoire littéraire de la France*, 13 (1906), 458–498 and 658–692.

3. On Belon, see Dr. Pierre Delaunay, "L'aventureuse existence de Pierre Belon du Mans," *Revue du XVIᵉ siècle* (1922), 251–268. Also (1923), 1–34, 125–147, and (1924), 30–48, 222–232 and (1925), 78–97, 256–268, 269–282.

4. This book is the source of Delaunay's reconstruction of Belon's travels and the basis of the portrait of the author presented in this chapter. References are to the 1555 edition (Anvers: Plantin). For Belon's other works, including the Latin edition of the *Observations*, see the catalogue of the Bibliothèque Nationale.

5. On La Boëtie, see Malcolm Smith, ed., *De la servitude volontaire* (Geneva: Droz, 1987).

6. On Muret, see Charles Dejob, *Muret* (Paris, 1881).

7. On Peletier, see Henri Chamard, *Histoire de la Pléiade*, 4 vols. (Paris, 1939–40), Pierre de Nolhac, *Ronsard et l'humanisme* (Paris: Champion, 1921), and André Boulanger's introduction to Peletier's *Art Poetique* (Paris, 1930).

8. See Nolhac, *Ronsard*.

9. Etienne Pasquier, *Les Oeuvres*, 2 vols. (Amsterdam, 1723). II, 2.

10. Belon, *Observations*, Introduction, 4, on "*utilité publique*"; "un bien est d'autent plus louable qu'il est commun"; on style: "j'ay traicté ceste mienne observation en nostre vulgaire François . . . n'usant d'autre artifice ou elegance d'oraison, sinon d'une forme simple."

11. Potez, *Deux années*, 687.

12. On Lambin's early life, see Potez, "La jeunesse de Denys Lambin," *Revue de l'histoire littéraire de la France*, 9 (1902), 385–413.

13. On Du Bellay, see the *Dictionnaire de Biographie Française*.

14. On the details of Belon's travels in Germany, see Delaunay. On Tournon, see Michel François, *Le Cardinal de Tournon* (Paris, 1951).

15. Belon, *Observations*, Preface, 2.

16. Ibid., 2v.

17. Ibid., Preface. Following the example of Democritus, he embarks on "lointaines peregrinations," and, like Ulysses, he expects to observe "la diversité des moeurs."

18. On André Thevet, see Frank Lestringant, *André Thevet* (Geneva: Droz, 1991).

19. André Thevet, *Cosmographie du Levant* (Lyon: Jean de Tournes, 1554), 16.

20. Ibid., 15.

21. Ibid., 36.

22. Belon, *Observations*, 7.

23. Ibid., 7v.

24. Ibid., 2, "les mesmes noms que les anciens autheurs nous ont laissé par escrit."

25. Ibid., 10v.

26. Ibid., 3.

27. Ibid., 7v.

28. Ibid., 67.

29. Loc. cit., "sçavoir acquis par l'estude."

30. Ibid., 2v. "profond sommeil d'ancienne ignorance."

31. Gilles was also a naturalist. He knew Greek and he was very much Belon's senior. At the time when Belon traveled in the Turkish empire, Gilles was close to 60. He was sent to the Levant, it seems, by King Francis himself, although he ended up, destitute, in Aleppo, having joined the Sultan's army for a time to make a living. He then traveled with Chesneau's party, which included the tempestuous orientalist Guillaume Postel, another genius of peasant background. Gilles and Postel did not get along, engaging, according to Chesneau, in bitter academic disputes on board as they sailed back to Constantinople. "Ils entroient souvent en dispute," reports Chesneau. "On avait bien affaire quelques fois à les mettre d'accord." Scheffer, *Voyage d'Aramon*, 139.

32. Belon, *Observations*, 272.

33. Scheffer, *Voyage d'Aramon*, 140.

34. See Ilana Zingler, "Narration et Témoignage dans les Observations de Pierre Belon." *Nouvelle Revue du Seizième Siècle*, 5 (1987), 25–40. The story, notes Zingler, of ancient origin, is reported in Pliny's Natural History and in Flavius Josephus' Jewish Wars. Talmudic tradition amplified the legend.

35. Belon, *Observations*, 257v. He is aware that Pliny reported the story. Presumably Pliny did not observe the phenomenon.

36. Loc. cit.

37. Ibid., 41–54, for the report on Lemnos clay.

38. Ibid., 78.

39. Ibid., 200v.

40. Ibid., 60v.

41. Ibid., 15.

42. Ibid., 178.

43. Ibid., 168v.

44. An anonymous pamphlet attributed to Osiander was published in 1540. It provided a rationalist critique of the popular belief in the special need of Jews for Christian blood. Both the Catholic theologian Eck and the Protestant theologian Luther attacked Osiander, defending the popular belief. This debate was a *cause célèbre* in Wittenberg while Belon was in residence there.

See Joy Margaret Kammerling, "Andreas Osiander and the Jews of Nuremberg: A Reformation Pastor and Jewish Toleration in Sixteenth Century Germany" (Ph.D. diss., University of Illinois at Chicago, 1995).

45. Belon, *Observations*, 110.

46. Ibid., 176.

47. Ibid., 248.

48. Ibid., 263. 49.

49. Ibid., 176. "Chose qui nous a bien servi, non seulement a nous interpreter, mais aussi à nous racompter les choses comme elles estoyent en ce pays là."

50. Thevet and Nicolay, the cartographer, express the crudest hostility toward non-Christians, especially Jews.

51. Belon, *Observations*, 77v.

52. Cicero, *De legibus* (London, New York: Loeb Classical Library, 1928), 328.

53. Belon, *Observations*, 50.

54. Ibid., 46v.

55. Ibid., 273.

56. Ibid., 273v.

57. Ibid., 106.

58. Ibid., 181.

59. Ibid., 62v.

60. Delauney (1925), 260.

61. Belon, *Observations*, 54v.

2. In Monsieur Brinon's Garden

1. Belon, *Observations*, 294v.

2. On Brinon, see Pierre de Nolhac, *Ronsard et l'humanisme* (Paris: Champion, 1921), 16. Among those who dedicated books to Brinon were the elderly and famous ambassador and classical scholar Lazare de Baïf and the young and reckless Marc Antoine Muret. Nolhac, 38.

3. Estienne Pasquier, *Recherches de la France*, in *Oeuvres*, Amsterdam, 1723, 2 vols. (Slatkine Reprints, 1971), II, 702. Pasquier records his reminiscences of that "belle guerre contre l'ignorance" some 50 years after the events in which he participated as a young man.

4. Nolhac, 16ff. Baïf also published translations of Euripides in the thirties and forties with the publisher Robert Estienne. See Lucien Pinvert, *Lazare de Baïf* (Paris, 1900).

5. For all this see Nolhac, *Ronsard*, and Henri Chamard, *Histoire de la Pléiade*, 4 vols. (Paris, 1939–40).

6. On Ramus' career, see Charles Waddington, *Ramus* (Paris, 1855; Slatkine Reprints, 1969).

7. Ramus, *Dialectique* (Paris, 1555), ed. Michel Dassonville (Geneva: Droz, 1964), 25. This quotation is from Ramus' *Scholae in liberales artes* (1569). It is cited in Dassonville's useful introduction to the *Dialectique*.

8. Ramus, *Dialectique*, 50: "les premiers hommes . . . ont pensé de Dialectique." Philosophie and Dialectique are used interchangeably by Ramus.

9. Ibid., 51.

10. Ramus' *Gramere* (Paris: Wechel, 1562), was written in his own phonetic spelling. He was on record as favoring the broadest possible access to education. Among other pronouncements on this topic, see his memorandum on the reforms which ought to be instituted in the University of Paris, *Advertissements sur la reformation de l'université de Paris au Roy* (Paris, 1562), 14. "C'est chose fort indigne que le chemin pour venir à la cognoissance de la Philosophie soit clos et deffendu à la povreté."

11. On this work, see Charles B. Schmitt, *Cicero Scepticus* (The Hague: Nijhoff, 1972).

12. On Péna, see Jean Dupèbe, "Autour du collège de Presles," *Bibliothèque d'Humanisme et Renaissance*, XLII (1980), 123–137, and R. Hooykaas, *Humanisme, Science et Réforme: Pierre de la Ramée (1515–1572)*, 45–46.

13. Castelnau's translation bore the title of *Traicté des façons et coutumes des anciens Gaulois* (Paris: Wechel, 1559). It was eventually reprinted in 1581, when Castelnau was ambassador in London, under a slightly different title, as *Traitté des meurs des anciens gaulois* (Paris: Denys du Val, 1581).

14. On Du Bellay's manifesto and the French translations of the optimi auctores by Ronsard et al., see Dassonville's introduction to the *Dialectique*, 8 and 64. Also Michel Dassonville, "La collaboration de la Pléiade à la Dialectique de Pierre de la Ramée," *Bibliothèque d'humanisme et Renaissance*, 25 (1983), 337–348.

15. Ramus, in the introduction to his *Gaulois*: "J'ayme mon pays." Pasquier, in the preface to his *Recherches*: "J'écris pour ma France."

16. On Tahureau, see Trevor Peach, *Nature et Raison. Etude critique des Dialogues de Jacques Tahureau* (Geneva: Slatkine, 1986). These dialogues were first published in 1565,

ten years after the author's death. The modern critical edition referred to here is Jacques Tahureau, *Les Dialogues*, ed. Max Gauna (Geneva: Droz, 1981). The opening comment cited here is on page 16. The background for Democritus as a philosopher who laughs at the human condition is in Horace, who is the prime inspiration of Ronsard's group and a key author of the parisian style.

17. Tahureau, *Dialogues*, 18.

18. Ibid., 13.

19. Ibid., 70 and 80.

20. Ibid., 83.

21. Ibid., 198.

22. Ibid., 129.

23. Ibid., 238.

24. Ibid., 231.

25. Ibid., 92.

26. Ibid., 125 on "cette quanaille," these "jappeurs," who cite Aristotle "pour approuver une Evangile."

27. Ibid., 129.

28. Ibid., 234.

29. Ibid., 240.

30. Ibid., 185. "Mesme" is Henri de Mesmes, who was also a student at Coqueret.

31. Max Gauna, *Upwellings. First Expressions of Unbelief in the Printed Literature of the French Renaissance* (Rutherford: Fairleigh Dickinson University Press, 1992). For the number of the Dialogues' edition, 205.

32. Louis Le Caron, *Dialogues*, ed. Joan Buhlman and Donald Gilman (Geneva: Droz, 1986).

33. "Je ne suis ne trop serf admirateur, ne trop arrogant despriseur de l'antiquité." *Dialogues*, 57.

34. Ibid., 67.

35. Ibid., 123.

36. Ibid., 90.

3. A School for Scandal

1. Estienne Pasquier, *Lettres* (Paris, 1619), II, 596.

2. Cited by Michel Dassonville in the introduction to his edition of Ramus' *Dialectique* of 1555 (Geneva: Droz, 1964), 22.

3. Ibid., 154: "cacqueter en l'eschole des reigles d'icelles."

4. Ibid., 22.

5. Antoine Loisel, *Opuscules* (Paris, 1656), 7.

6. Pierre Galland, *Pro Schola Parisiensis* (Paris, 1551). Cited by Henri Busson, *Le rationalisme dans la littérature française de la Renaissance* (Paris, 1957), 35.

7. Ibid., 42.

8. See Pierre de Nolhac, *Ronsard et l'humanisme* (Paris: Champion, 1921).

9. See George Huppert, *Public Schools in Renaissance France* (Urbana: University of Illinois Press, 1984).

10. Peter Sharrat, "N. Nancelius, Petri Rami Vita," *Humanistica Lovanensia*, XXIV (1975).

11. See Huppert, *Public Schools in Renaissance France.*

12. Ramus, *Dialectique*, 9.

13. Ramus, *Advertissements sur la reformation de l'université de Paris, au roy* (Paris, 1562), 14: "C'est chose fort indigne que le chemin pour venir à la cognoissance de la Philosophie soit clos et deffendu a la povreté, encores qu'elle feust docte."

14. Ramus, *Dialectique*, 8, n.8.

15. Ibid., 52.

16. Cicero, *De natura deorum* (London, New York: Loeb Classical Library), 3–4.

17. Charles B. Schmitt, *Cicero Scepticus* (The Hague, 1972), 83.

18. Ibid., 78.

19. Ibid., 64, n.100.

20. Ibid., 92.

21. Ibid., 86.

22. Ibid., 84.

23. Ibid., 96–97.

24. Ramus, *Advertissements*, 33.

25. Schmitt, *Cicero Scepticus*, 92.

26. Ramus, *Dialectique* (Paris, 1577 ed.), Introduction, unpaginated.

27. Charles Waddington, *Ramus* (Paris, 1855), 195 and 229.

28. Ramus, *Dialectique*, 50: "les premiers hommes . . . ont pensé de Dialectique." 52: Galien a esté le dernier . . . et en a fermé la porte."

29. Ibid., 155.

30. Ibid., 99.

31. Schmitt, *Cicero Scepticus*, 93.

32. For this practice, we can refer not only to the published writings of Ramus and Talon, but to the testimony of the college's alumni. See, for instance, the reminiscences of Antoine Loisel, who spent five years in Ramus's college and afterward remained close enough to Ramus to be named executor of his will. Loisel was to remember that his instructor, master Amariton, "traittoit alors la Philosophie d'une maniere assez nouvelle, l'interpretant par les Epistres d'Horace (*Opuscules* [Paris, 1656], p. 7).

33. Ramus, *Dialectique*, 24.

34. Ibid., 154. ". . . il les faut exercer [the rules of reasoning] ès poëtes, orateurs, philosophes. . .en imitant premierement leur bonne invention . . . et puis taschant les esgaller, voire surmonter en traitant et disputant de toutes choses par soy mesme et sans plus avoir egard à leurs disputes" (p. 154).

35. Waddington, *Ramus*, 74.

36. Ibid., 26.

37. Ramus, *Dialectique*, 8.

38. Ibid., 9.

39. For a typical attitude in this regard, see Geneviève Demerson, *Dorat* (Clermont: Adosa, 1983), p. 257.

40. *Petri Rami professoris regii . . . praefationes . . .* (Paris, 1577), p. 148. Cited in Waddington, *Ramus*, p. 14.

41. Waddington, *Ramus*, p. 54. For a copy of the court order, see Bibliothèque Nationale, ms. Dupuy 581, 119, "Arrest de la cour contre Villon, Bidault et Declaves pour avoir proposé des theses en public contre les dogmes d'Aristotle et autres mauvaises propositions."

The court order demands that, following the complaint of the "doyen, syndics et docteurs de la faculté de Theologie," the three men guilty of having spoken against Aristotle are to leave Paris within 24 hours and are forbidden to settle anywhere within the jurisdiction of the *parlement* and, of course, are forbidden to teach philosophy in any university within this jurisdiction. Further, all persons "de quelque estat, qualité ou condition qu'ils soient" are forbidden to discuss the propositions contained in these theses, "sous peine de punition corporelle," and finally, as the court works up to a higher level of indignation, it "faict deffence à toutes personnes, sous peine de la vie, enseigner aucune maxime" against Aristotle or otherwise unapproved by the doctors of the theology faculty.

I doubt that these prohibitions resulted in any actual legal action against anyone in particular, in the general confusion and bizarre climate of opinion of 1624, but the desire to intimidate is obviously very much alive, and the court lends itself to the hallucinatory intrigues of the theology faculty and of the Jesuit and Minime fathers who, in daily public sermons, call for mob action against dangerous intellectuals. See F. Lachèvre, *Le procès du poète Thèophile de Viau* (Paris: Champion, 1909).

42. *Lettres* (Paris, 1619): ". . . je seray tousjours du party de ceux qui suivront le grand chemin de la raison" (p. 27). The letter was written in 1555, the year of the publication of Ramus's *Dialectique*.

43. From a letter written by Pasquier in 1552 to the great classicist Turnèbe: ". . . je m'asseure que tout homme de bon jugement sera d'accord avec moy, que nous devons estudier les langues, non point à cause d'elles, ains pour les disciplines" (p. 12).

44. Pasquier, *Lettres* (1586), 7. Pasquier speaks contemptuously of ". . . un certain sçavoir pedantesque de plusieurs qui font estat d'apprendre le Grec, non pour tirer la moëlle qui est aux oeuvres de Platon et d'Aristotle, ains, sans plus, pour discourir sur le dialecte d'un mot."

45. Michel de Montaigne, *Essais* in *Oeuvres complètes de Montaigne*, Pléiade ed. (Paris: Gallimard, 1962), p. 236.

46. Pasquier writes, ". . . je vous prie, ne soyons, vous et moy, preoccupez d'un respect que par fois avec trop de superstition nous portons à l'ancienneté" (*Recherches de la France*, in *Oeuvres*, 2 vols. [Paris, 1723], p. 645; hereafter cited as *Recherches*).

47. Pasquier, *Lettres* (1619), 101: ". . . faire teste à toutes les anciennes propositions de ceux qui se sont estimez les plus sages." He adds, for good measure: ". . . tous ces vieux resveurs qui se donnerent le nom et tiltre de Philosophes, n'estoyent gens sages."

48. See Pasquier, *Lettres*, p. 95, on being a *philosophe* who is a *citoyen du monde*; see his homage to the memory of Ramus regarding the need for the *philosophe* to be *un homme d'estat* (". . . en enseignant la jeunesse, il estoit un homme d'Estat" [*Recherches*, p. 838]).

4. Liberté, Egalité, Fraternité

1. References are to the modern edition, Estienne de La Boëtie, *De la servitude volontaire*, ed. Malcolm Smith (Geneva: Droz, 1987).

2. *Servitude*, Introduction, 18.

3. Ibid., 10, and Michel de Montaigne, *Essais*, in *Oeuvres complètes*, 193 (De l'amitié).

4. See Paul Bonnefon, *Oeuvres complètes d'Estienne de la Boëtie* (Geneva: Slatkine Reprints, 1967), xiii–lxxxv.

5. Bonnefon, lxxiii.

6. *Servitude*, 22.

7. Ibid., 24.

8. Ibid., 41.

9. Ibid., 41.

10. Ibid., 42.

11. Ibid., 35.

12. Ibid., 38: "C'est le peuple qui s'asservit."

13. Ibid., 39.

14. Ibid., 41.

15. Ibid., 45; 51: "La premiere raison de la servitude volontaire c'est la coutume."

16. Ibid., 47.

17. Ibid., 47.

18. Ibid., 51.

19. Ibid., 56–57.

20. Ibid., 58.

21. Ibid., 62.

22. Ibid., 52.

23. Ibid., 52.

24. Ibid., 66–68. The word "mange-peuples" may be borrowed from Rabelais. See M. A. Screech, *Rabelais* (Ithaca: Cornell University Press, 1979), 224, on Rabelais' coinage of "demovore."

25. References are to the French version by Michel de Castelnau.

26. Pierre de La Ramée, *Traicté des façons et coustumes des anciens gaulois* (Paris, 1559). In the dedication, Ramus confesses: "J'ayme mon païs" and speaks of the "partie morale de l'histoire de mon païs." This is on page 5.

27. *Traicté* (1581 edition), 62.

28. Ibid., 7v.

29. Ibid., 9v.

30. See George Huppert, *The Idea of Perfect History* (Urbana, Chicago, London: University of Illinois Press, 1970), Appendix II.

31. Ramus, *Traicté* (1581), 19v.

32. Ibid., 8v.

33. Ibid., 9.

34. Ibid., 12v–13r.

35. Ibid., 61v.

36. Ibid., 14v.

37. Ibid., 20v.

38. Ibid., 20v.

39. Ibid., 22.

40. Ibid., 22.

41. Ibid., 9v.

42. Ibid., *Traicté* (1559 edition), 57.

43. Ibid., 19.

44. Ibid., 76v.

45. Ibid., 93.

46. Ibid., 95; "si le Prince eut fait autrement, il n'eut eu aucune autorité."

5. Historical Research in the Service of Philosophy

1. Jean Dupèbe, "Autour du collège de Presles," *Bibliothèque d'Humanisme et Renaissance*, XLII (1980), 123–147, 128.

2. An excellent modern critical edition was provided by Enea Balmas (Milan, 1957).

3. *Des Recherches de la France Livre Premier, Plus un Pourparler du Prince. Le Tout par Estienne Pasquier, advocat en la Cour de Parlement de Paris pour Vincent Sertenas, tenant sa boutique au Palais et en la rue neuve nostre Dame, à l'enseigne St. Jean l'Evangeliste* (Paris, 1560).

4. Ibid., "Au Lecteur." Pasquier's show of independence is muted. He did not dedicate his book to a patron, but he sent a copy to the Cardinal de Lorraine with a covering letter full of the usual compliments. Even in his letter to the Cardinal, it is true, he departs from the usual, excessive formulas of politeness current at Court and signs his letter with a simple: "A Dieu." The letter was eventually published together with many other letters of Pasquier. References, unless otherwise indicated, are to the 1723 edition of Pasquier's *Oeuvres complètes* in 2 volumes, reprinted by Slatkine in 1971, II, 27. The simple "A Dieu" was, for Pasquier, a salutation as democratic as the Roman "Vale." See the letter to his close friend and classmate at Presles, Antoine Loisel. Pasquier was determined to get rid of excessive compliments, "ces mots de Monseigneur, Monsieur & autres" and other forms of "perte de temps et remplissage de papier" (*Oeuvres*, II, 2).

5. *Oeuvres*, II, 12.

6. *Lettres* (1619), II, 596. See the 1723 edition, II, 606.

7. *Oeuvres*, I, 1. For a detailed discussion of Pasquier's innovations and his place in the history of historiography, see Huppert, *Idea of Perfect History*.

8. Ibid., I, 2.

9. Ibid., I, 3.

10. *Oeuvres*, II, 10.

11. Ibid., I, 3.

12. Ibid., II, 9.

13. Ibid., II, 630. In this letter he describes his habit of meeting with master Beguin, principal of the collège du Cardinal Lemoine and master Le Vasseur, principal of the collège de Reims. They would meet regularly, going for walks in the suburbs and gardens just behind the hill, talking about Scripture, philosophy, and history.

14. See Huppert, *Idea of Perfect History*.

15. La Boëtie, *Servitude* (Bonnefon edition of *Oeuvres complètes*), 42.

16. See Huppert, *Idea of Perfect History*, ch. 4.

17. Pasquier, *Lettres* (1619), I, 107.

18. Pasquier, *Oeuvres*, I, 17: "ne sçavent où ils en sont."

19. Ibid., I, 17: "à la traverse."

20. Ibid., I, 17: "aucune mention en Cesar, Pline, Tacite, Ptolemée ou Strabon."

21. Ibid., I, 19: "quel autheur ancien?"; 23: "ruine provint de Constantine"; 24: "ces Empereurs usoient, si je ne m'abuse, plus de la Religion pour la commodité de leurs affaires, que par zèle ou devotion."

22. Ibid., I, 19.

23. Ibid., I, 6: "connoissant le danger qui escherroit . . . à celuy qui voudrait entreprendre d'escrire une histoire moderne."

24. Anonymous, *Les Recherches des Recherches et autres oeuvres de Mr. E. Pasquier, pour la defense de nos Roys, contre les outrages, calomnies et autres impertinences dudict Autheur* (Paris: S. Chappelet, 1622).

25. Pasquier, *Oeuvres*, II, 12.

26. Ibid., II, 45 ("nostre langue symbolize ordinairement avec nos moeurs").

27. Ibid., II, 55–62.

28. Ibid., II, 654.

29. Ibid., II, 289.

30. Ibid., II, 256.

31. Ibid., II, 33.

32. Ibid., II, 6.

33. Ibid., I, 646.

34. Ibid., II, 67.

35. Garasse, *Recherches*, title page.

36. Pasquier, *Oeuvres*, II, 266.

37. Ibid., II, 267.

38. Ibid., I, 172.

39. Ibid., I, 663–664.

40. Garasse, *Recherches*, 681.

41. Ibid., 683.

42. Ibid., 683.

43. Garasse, *La doctrine curieuse des beaux esprits de ce temps ou pretendus tels* (Paris, 1624), 144.

44. Jean Descaurres, *Oeuvres morales* (Paris, 1584), 536v, also 128v–129.

45. Ibid., 194.

46. Garasse, *Doctrine*, 27.

47. Garasse, *Recherches*, 79.

48. Huppert, *Idea of Perfect History*, 41.

49. Ibid., 173.

50. Garasse, *Recherches*, 87.

51. Ibid., 96.

52. Garasse, *Doctrine*, 21.

53. Garasse, *Recherches*, 692.

54. Ibid., 720, "amphibie d'esprit."

55. Ibid., 150.

56. Garasse, *Doctrine*, 144.

57. See n.43 above.

58. Garasse, *Doctrine*, Au lecteur.

59. Marin Mersenne, *L'impiété des Deistes, Athées et Libertins de ce temps* (Paris, 1624), Preface, unpaginated. "Ces braves reformateurs ne jugent personne et croyent que chacun sera sauvé en sa religion, aussi bien le Turc et le Juif comme le réformé."

60. Ibid., 171.

61. Ibid., 173.

62. Ibid., 238.

63. Ibid., Preface. "C'est ce qui te fera brusler."

64. Garasse, *Doctrine*, 2.

6. *Optimi Auctores*

1. Anonymous, *Advis à Messieurs de l'Assemblée* (Paris, 1627), 7.

2. For a detailed study of this development, see Huppert, *Public Schools in Renaissance France.*

3. G. Codina-Mir, S.J., *Aux sources de la pédagogie des Jesuites: le modus parisiensis* (Rome, 1968), 52.

4. Pierre Charron, *De la sagesse*. References are to the collected works, *Toutes les oeuvres* (Paris, 1635). Marin Mersenne's *L'impiété des Deistes, Athées et Libertins* (Paris, 1624) is dedicated to Richelieu.

5. Charron, *Sagesse*, 182.

6. Ibid., Preface.

7. Loc. cit.

8. Ibid., 64.

9. Ibid., 65.

10. Ibid., 64.

11. That is the thesis of Codina-Mir in the work cited in n.3, above.

12. See Ernest Gaullieur, *Histoire du collège de Guyenne* (Paris, 1879).

13. Ibid., 1 on printer's contract; 4 on watery houses.

14. The contract is published by Gaullieur, 29–31. For student body size, see Roger Trinquet, *La jeunesse de Montaigne* (Paris, 1972), 465.

15. Gaullieur, 34.

16. Trinquet, 481.

17. Trinquet is suggestive in this regard.

18. This is what Pasquier was doing just then.

19. See F. Belin, *Histoire de l'université de Provence* (Paris: Picard, 1896), vol. 1, 273.

20. A. Prudhomme, "L'enseignement secondaire à Grenoble," *Bulletin de l'Academie Delphinale* 14 (1900), 93–139. See Grenoble, Archives municipales, BB.13.

21. Grenoble, Archives municipales, BB.15.

22. Ernest Bouchard, *Histoire du collège de Moulins* (Moulins, 1872), 9. Bouchard cites the city's contract with the sieur Raillet of 27 April 1556, "pour régler le collège comme ceux de Paris." It should be pointed out that provincial officials refer to the Parisian style as a model as early as the 1530s when there were as yet probably no colleges in Paris functioning according to the new model. Why then do advocates of educational reform speak of *le stile de Paris?*

The answer, I believe, has to do with the unique position of Paris as Europe's largest university town. Paris attracted academic talent from everywhere. Dutchmen like Erasmus, Spaniards like Loyola, Italians, Germans, Flemings, Scots all flocked to the Latin Quarter, joining legions of bright adolescents from Picardy, Normandy, and Provence.

Newly minted masters of arts, their heads filled with new ideas not necessarily picked up in the classroom, were eager to sign contracts with cities willing to employ them. Wherever they signed on, they introduced the new style of education which in Paris may still have been in an experimental stage.

Before it was institutionalized and written into contracts which specified which *auctores* must be read in which class, the outlines of the new style were lodged in the minds of hundreds of underemployed masters of arts.

23. J. Gardère, "Les écoles de Condom," *Revue de Gascogne* 26 (1885), 483.

24. Geneviève Durtelle de St. Sauveur, "Le collège de Rennes," *Bulletin et mémoires de la société archéologique d'Ile et Vilaine* (1918), 28.

7. Dangerous Classes

1. Léon Ménard, *Histoire de Nîmes*, 7 vols. (Paris, 1744–1758), IV, 134–135.

2. Henri Hauser, *Etudes sur la réforme française* (Paris, 1909), 19.

3. P. Imbart de la Tour, *Les origines de la réforme*, 2 vols. (Paris, 1905).

4. M. O. Fallières and Chanoine Durengues, "Enquêtes sur les commencements du Protestantisme en Agenais" in *Recueil des travaux de la société d'agriculture d'Agen* (1913), 16, 213–386.

5. On Cordier, see Jules Le Coultre, *Mathurin Cordier* (Neuchâtel, 1926).

6. See Huppert, *Public Schools in Renaissance France*, 100.

7. Waddington, *Ramus*, 244.

8. Ménard, *Nîmes,* IV, 298.

9. Aneau's contract with the city, for 1588, is in Lyon, Archives municipales, BB.81, ff. 91–94. On Tournon's strategy, see Michel François, *Le Cardinal de Tournon* (Paris, 1951), 396.

10. Huppert, *Public Schools in Renaissance France*, 132–133.

11. Ménard, *Nîmes*, IV, and Abbé Goiffon, *L'instruction publique à Nîmes* (Nîmes, 1876).

12. Codina-Mir, *Sources*, 52.

13. For all this see François, *Tournon*.

14. For Troyes, see Gustave Carré, *L'enseignement secondaire à Troyes* (Paris, 1888).

15. Laon, *Archives municipales*, BB.30.

16. Gaullieur, *Bordeaux*.

8. *Ex Tenebras Lux*

1. Frédéric Lachèvre, *Le procés de Théophile de Viau* (Paris: Champion, 1909), xvi.

2. Ibid., 207.

3. Ibid., xvi.

4. Molière, *Tartuffe*, Act I, scene 5, in Donald Frame's translation (New York: New American Library, 1967.)

5. Here I tend to share the conclusions of Olivier René Bloch, who doubts that the stereotype of the *libertin* created by controversialists like Garasse and Mersenne corresponds to anything real. See Bloch, *La philosophie de Gassendi* (The Hague, 1971), p. xv.

6. Huppert, *Public Schools in Renaissance France*, 116.

7. Cited in Alain Niderst, *Fontenelle à la recherche de lui-même (1657–1702)* (Paris, 1972), 296.

8. F. de Dainville, *L'education des Jésuites* (Paris, 1978), 129.

9. Ibid., 134.

10. Huppert, *Public Schools in Renaissance France*, 128.

11. "Poeta-philosophus" is the admiring epithet employed by the philosopher Gassendi when speaking of Horace, while Garasse calls Pasquier the "*cousin-germain*" of Horace.

12. On the printing history and popularity of Montaigne, see the Introduction to the Pléiade edition of the *Oeuvres complètes*.

13. All the works of the *auctores* circulated in French translation, including works as provocative as Cicero's *De natura deorum* (as early as 1581), or the collected sayings of

Plutarch, Seneca, Socrates, and Epictetus (*Les morales*, Paris, 1667), or the complete *Oeuvres* of Seneca translated by Mathieu de Chalvet (Paris, 1604; Rouen, 1634).

14. Pierre Gassendi, *Dissertations en forme de paradoxes contre les Aristotéliens* (Paris: Vrin, 1959, Bernard Rochot transl. and ed.), 100, "mon cher Charron," "surtout grâce à Ramus."

15. See Bloch, *Philosophie de Gassendi.*

16. Gassendi, *Dissertations*, Introduction.

17. Gassendi, *Dissertations*, 100.

18. Ibid., 100, 106b, 111a.

19. Cyrano de Bergerac, *Oeuvres diverses* (Paris, 1654), 81.

20. See the preface to his letters, Pierre Bayle, *Oeuvres diverses*, 4 vols. in fol. (The Hague, 1737), I, 7.

21. See Pierre Rétat, *Le dictionnaire de Bayle et la lutte philosophique au 18ᵉᵐᵉ siècle* (Paris, 1974), 16.

22. Dictionaire, I, article "Démocrite."

23. Descaurres, *Oeuvres*, 125v.

24. Bayle, *Oeuvres*, III, 110.

25. Ibid., 114.

26. Rétat, *Le dictionnaire*, 244.

27. A most succinct version of this standard philosophical *Erziehungsroman* can be found in Gabriel Naudé's *Considérations politiques sur les coups d'état*, which takes its place between Gassendi and Bayle. "I went through the scholastic philosophy without becoming disputatious," writes Naudé, "and read both the ancient and the modern philosophers without taking sides, not having taken an oath, after all, to follow the opinion of any authority. Seneca has done more for me than Aristotle, Plutarch more than Plato, Juvenal and Horace more than Homer and Virgil. As for Montaigne and Charron, they meant more to me than all those writers I just mentioned." (In the modern edition, Paris, 1988), 5, page 81.

28. Niderst, *Fontenelle*, 48–50.

29. Ibid., 48.

30. Ibid., 51.

31. Ibid., 55.

32. Ibid., 61.

33. Ibid., 112.

34. Ibid., 113.

35. Ibid., 191.

36. For this and everything else concerning the lively intellectual salons of the early seventeenth century, see the encyclopedic work of René Pintard, *Le libertinage érudit* (Paris, 1943; Geneva: Slatkine Reprints, 1983).

37. A case in point—granted, an uncommon one—is that of the Morel family. Jean de Morel, who had been a student of Dorat and who had lived in Basel, near Erasmus, whom he admired, was a high-level adviser of the chancellor Olivier. Morel's wife, Antoinette de Loynes, knew Latin. The Morel salon, on the rue Pavée, was a rallying point for the avant-garde and the cultivated humanists, perhaps even more so than the country estate of Jean Brinon. The Morels had three daughters, who were tutored at home by a distinguished scholar from Ghent. One of the girls, Camille, spoke Greek at 10, knew how to write Hebrew letters, and sang, accompanying herself on the lute, Ronsard's poems set to music. Du Bellay, Buchanan, and Dorat dedicated poems to Camille whose own poems were published as well. See Pierre de Nolhac, *Ronsard et l'humanisme* (Paris: Champion, 1921), 170–177.

38. This did not fool his contemporaries, nor did it impress careful scholars later on, including Waddington and Dupèbe, who worked with indisputable archival sources, but

it was enough to convince a literary theorist like Father Ong, S.J., that Ramus "came of a noble family." See W. J. Ong, *Ramus and the Decline of Rhetoric* (Cambridge, 1958), 18.

39. See George Huppert, "Lucullus, Crassus and Cato in Grenoble," *Historical Reflections* XV, 1 (1988), 271–278.

40. Huppert, *Public Schools in Renaissance France*, 130–140, "Small Town Schools."

41. See George Huppert, *After the Black Death* (Bloomington: Indiana University Press, 1986).

42. Maurice Dommanget, *Le curé Meslier* (Paris, 1965).

43. Jean Meslier, *Oeuvres complètes*, 3 vols., ed. J. Deprun, R. Desné, and A. Soboul (Paris, 1970).

44. *Etudes sur Meslier* (Paris, 1966) and *Le curé Meslier* (Reims, 1980). These are collections of papers presented on the occasion of scholarly meetings devoted to Meslier, the earlier one at Aix, the later at Reims.

45. Meslier, *Oeuvres*, I, 7. "Dès ma plus tendre jeunesse."

46. Dommanget, *Meslier*, 19.

47. Michel Devèze, "Les villages et la région" in *Le curé Meslier* (Reims, 1980).

48. Nicole Perrin, "La vie religieuse," ibid.

49. Meslier, *Oeuvres*, I, 5.

50. Ibid., 38.

51. Ibid., 5–42. Numbers in brackets refer to page numbers in the Avant-Propos.

52. "Tous les hommes sont égaux par la nature . . ." Meslier's source appears to be Seneca. See Meslier, *Textes* (Paris, 1973, Roland Desné, ed.), 73.

53. Meslier, *Oeuvres*, I, 8–9.

54. Ibid., 34–35. "Deicoles" is Meslier's term for believers.

55. Ibid., 23–24.

56. Meslier, *Oeuvres*, III, 147–148.

57. Meslier, *Textes*, 73.

58. Meslier, *Oeuvres*, III, 159.

59. Montaigne, *Essais*, 358. As Henri Weber points out, Meslier distorts the meaning here, to serve his purposes, but he is adept at reading between the lines and may well have reconstructed Montaigne's hidden intention. Weber, in *Etudes sur Meslier* (Paris, 1966), 53.

60. "*Tantum religio potuit suadere malorum.*" See Weber, op. cit. 58. For his ownership of the *Essais*, see Dommanget, *Meslier*, 147.

61. Dommanget, *Meslier*, 75.

62. Ibid., 177. Meslier used an edition of 1715. References here are to the 1710 edition in six volumes. The author, J. P. Marana, died in 1693.

63. *L'Espion*, II, 14.

64. Ibid., II, 36.

65. Ibid., II, 35.

66. Ibid., II, 34.

67. Ibid., II, 204.

68. Ibid., II, 364.

69. Ibid., III, 301.

70. Ibid., III, 140–141.

71. Ibid., VI, 179.

72. Ibid., VI, 178.

73. Montaigne, *Essais*, 613.

74. *L'Espion*, IV, 19.

75. Ibid., V, 83.

76. Jean Descaurres, *Oeuvres morales* (Paris, 1584), 113v–114.

77. *L'Espion Turc*, IV, 180.

78. This passage from Jefferson's letter is cited by Gary McDowell in the *Times Literary Supplement* (June 1995), page 7.

9. The Republic of Letters

1. Cited by Waddington, *Ramus*, title page.

2. Rétat, *Le dictionnaire de Bayle*, 260.

3. In the preface to the first volume, Amsterdam, 1684.

4. Adrienne Koch and William Peden, eds., *The Life and Selected Writings of Thomas Jefferson* (New York: Random House, 1944), p. 374.

5. See Charles G. Nauert, Jr., *Humanism and the Culture of Renaissance Europe* (Cambridge: Cambridge University Press, 1995), especially page 111. Also James H. Overfield, *Humanism and Scholasticism in Late Medieval Germany* (Princeton, 1984), and Charles Nauert, "Humanist Infiltration into the Academic World," *Renaissance Quarterly* 43 (1990), 799–812.

6. Cited by Olivier René Bloch, *La philosophie de Gassendi* (The Hague, 1971), 54.

7. Bloch, *Gassendi*, 42–43. See also René Pintard, *Le libertinage érudit dans la première moitié du XVII* siècle (Geneva/Paris: Slatkine Reprints, 1983), 147–156.

8. Bloch, *Gassendi*, 58.

BIBLIOGRAPHY

Primary Sources

Agrippa, Henry Cornelius. *Declamation sur l'incertitude des sciences.* Translated by Louis Turquet de Mayerne. Paris: J. Durand, 1582.

Anonymous. *Advis à Messieurs de l'Assemblée.* Paris: n.p., 1627.

Anonymous (Garasse). *Les Recherches des Recherches et autres oeuvres de Mr. E. Pasquier, pour la defense de nos Roys, contre les outrages, calomnies et autres impertinences dudict Autheur.* Paris: S. Chappelet, 1622.

Bayle, Pierre. *Choix de correspondance inédite.* Edited by E. Gigas. Copenhagen: Gad, 1890.

———. *Dictionaire historique et critique.* 2 vols. in folio. Rotterdam: Rainier Leers, 1697.

———. *Oeuvres diverses.* 4 vols. in folio. The Hague: Compagnie des Libraires, 1737.

Bergerac, Cyrano de. *Oeuvres diverses.* Paris: C. de Sercy, 1654.

Bernier, François. *Abrégé de la philosophie de Gassendi.* 7 vols. Lyon: Anisson, 1684.

Bruès, Guy de. *Dialogues.* Baltimore: The Johns Hopkins Press, 1953.

Budé, Guillaume. *L'étude des lettres.* Edited and translated by M.M. de la Garanderie. (This is a critical edition of Budé's *De studio literarum recte et commode instituendo,* Paris, 1532.) Paris: Les Belles Lettres, 1988.

Castellion, Sebastien. *De l'art de douter.* Geneva: Editions Jeheber, 1953.

Charron, Pierre. *De la sagesse.* In *Toutes les oeuvres.* Paris: J. Villery, 1635.

Chesneau, Jean. *Le Voyage de M. d'Aramon.* Edited by Charles Scheffer. Paris: E. Leroux, 1887.

Cicero. *Academica.* M. T. Ciceronis Academicorum Liber Primus. Paris: Garnier, 1872.

———. *De legibus.* Loeb Classical Library. Cambridge: Harvard University Press, 1928.

———. *De la Nature des Dieux.* Translated by Guy Le Fevre de la Boderie. Paris: L'Angelier, 1581.

———. *De natura deorum.* Loeb Classical Library. Cambridge: Harvard University Press, 1933.

Descaurres, Jean. *Oeuvres morales.* Paris: G. de la Noue, 1584.

Des Périers, Bonaventure. *Cymbalum Mundi.* Geneva: Droz, 1983.

Estienne, Henri. *Apologie pour Hérodote.* 2 vols. Paris: Lisieux, 1879.

François I. "Lettres patentes du Roy François I contre Pierre Ramus, pour avoir composé quelques livres contre la doctrine d'Aristote, 10 mars 1543." Bibliothèque Nationale, manuscrits, Collection Dupuy. Vol. 518, ff. 113–15.

Galland, Pierre. *Pro Schola Parisiensis.* Paris: 1551. Quoted in Henri Busson, *Le rationalisme dans la littérature française de la Renaissance.* Paris: 1957, 35.

Garasse, François. *La doctrine curieuse des beaux esprits de ce temps ou pretendus tels.* Paris: S. Chappelet, 1624.

Gassendi, Pierre. *Dissertations en forme de paradoxes contre les Aristotéliens.* Translated and edited by Bernard Rochot. Paris: J. Vrin, 1959.

La Boëtie, Estienne de. *De la servitude volontaire.* Edited by Malcolm Smith. Geneva: Droz, 1987.

———. *Mémoire sur la pacification des Troubles.* Geneva: Droz, 1983.

La Mothe Le Vayer, François de. *Quatre Dialogues.* Francfort: J. Sarius: 1604.

Le Caron, Louis. *Dialogues*. Edited by Joan Buhlman and Donald Gilman. Geneva: Droz, 1986.

Loisel, Antoine. *Opuscules*. Paris: J. Guignard, 1656.

Marana, J. P. *L'espion dans les cours des princes chrétiens*. 6 vols. Cologne: E. Kinkius, 1710.

Mersenne, Marin. *L'impiété des Deistes, Athées et Libertins de ce temps*. 2 vols. Paris: P. Bilaine, 1624.

Meslier, Jean. *Oeuvres complètes*. Edited by J. Deprun, R. Desné and A. Soboul. 3 vols. Paris: Editions Anthropos, 1970–72.

———. *Textes*. Edited by Roland Desné. Paris: L'Oeil Ouvert, 1973.

Molière (Jean Baptiste Poquelin). *Tartuffe*. Translated by Donald Frame. New York: New American Library, 1967.

Montaigne, Michel de. *Essais*. In *Oeuvres complètes de Montaigne*. Paris: Gallimard, 1962.

Naudé, Gabriel. *Considérations politiques sur les coups d'état*. Paris: n.p., 1667.

Nicolai, Friedrich. *Uber meine gelehrte Bildung*. Berlin: n.p., 1799.

Pasquier, Estienne. *Les Oeuvres*. 2 vols. in folio. Amsterdam: Compagnie des Libraires, 1723.

———. *Lettres*. Paris: L. Sonnius, 1619.

Perrault, Charles. *Mémoires*. Edited by Paul Bonnefon. Paris: H. Laurens, 1909.

Peletier, Jacques. *L'Art Poëtique*. Paris: Les Belles Lettres, 1930.

Plutarch. *Les morales de Plutarque, Seneque, Socrate, Epictète*. Paris: G. Tompere, 1667.

Ramus, Petrus (Pierre de la Ramée). *Advertissements sur la reformation de l'université de Paris, au Roy*. Paris: n.p., 1562.

———. *Dialectique*. Avignon: Bonhomme, 1556.

———. *Dialectique*. [Paris: 1555.] Edited by Michel Dassonville. Geneva: Droz, 1964.

———. *Gramere*. Paris: A. Wechel, 1562.

———. *La Dialectique de M. Pierre de La Ramée*. Paris: G. Auvray, 1577.

———. *Petri Rami professoris regii (et. A. Talei) collectanae praefationes, epistolae, orationes*. Paris: apud D. Vallensem, 1577.

———. *Traicté des façons et coutumes des anciens Gaulois*. Translated by Michel de Castelnau. Paris: Wechel, 1559.

Ronsard, Pierre. "Des vertus Intellectuelles et morales," in *Oeuvres complètes*. 2 vols. Edited by G. Cohen. Paris: Gallimard, 1950.

Lucian. *Les Oeuvres*. Translated by J. Baudoin. Paris: J. Richer, 1613.

Seneca. *Les Oeuvres*. Rouen: J. Behourt, 1634.

Spinoza, Baruch. *Oeuvres*. 2 vols. Paris: Garnier, 1928.

Tahureau, Jacques. *Les Dialogues*. Edited by Max Gauna. Geneva: Droz, 1981.

Thevet, André. *Cosmographie du Levant*. Lyon: Jean de Tournes, 1554.

Turquet de Mayerne, Louis. *La monarchie aristo-democratique*. Paris: J. Berjon, 1611.

Secondary Sources

Adam, Antoine. *Les libertins au 17ᵉᵐᵉ siècle*. Paris: Buchet/Chastel, 1964.

Belin, F. *Histoire de l'université de Provence*. Paris: Picard, 1896.

Bloch, Olivier. "Quelques aspects de la tradition libertine." *Romanistische Zeitschrift für Literaturgeschichte* 13 (1989): 61–63.

Bouchard, Ernest. *Histoire du collège de Moulins*. Moulins: Desrosiers, 1872.

Buisson, Ferdinand. *Sébastien Castellion*. 2 vols. Paris: Hachette, 1892.

Busson, Henri. *Le rationalisme dans la littérature française de la Renaissance*. Paris: J. Vrin, 1957.

Carré, Gustave. *L'enseignement secondaire à Troyes*. Paris: Hachette, 1888.

Chamard, Henri. *Histoire de la Pléiade*. 4 vols. Paris: H. Didier, 1939–40.

Clément, Louis. *Henri Estienne et son oeuvre française*. Paris: Picard, 1899.

Codina-Mir, G., S.J. *Aux sources de la pédagogie des Jesuites: le modus parisiensis*. Rome: Institutum Historicum S.I., 1968.

Dainville, F. de. *L'education des Jésuites*. Paris: Editions de Minuit, 1978.

Dassonville, Michel. "La collaboration de la Pléiade à la Dialectique de Pierre de la Ramée." *Bibliothèque d'humanisme et Renaissance*, 25 (1983): 337–348.

Dejob, Charles. *Muret*. Paris: E. Thorin, 1881.

Delaunay, Dr. Pierre. "L'aventureuse existence de Pierre Belon du Mans." *Revue du XVIe siècle* (1922): 251–268; (1923): 1–34; 125–147; (1924): 30–48, 222–232; (1925): 78–97; 256–268; 269–282.

Demerson, Geneviève. *Dorat*. Clermont: Adosa, 1983.

Devèze, Michel. "Les villages et la région" in *Le curé Meslier*. Reims: Bibliothèque de l'Université de Reims, 1980.

Dommanget, Maurice. *Le curé Meslier*. Paris: Julliard, 1965.

Dupèbe, Jean. "Autour du collège de Presles." *Bibliothèque d'Humanisme et Renaissance*, XLII (1980): 123–137.

Durtelle de St. Sauveur, Geneviève. "Le collège de Rennes," *Bulletin et mémoires de la société archéologique d'Ile et Vilaine* (1918), 28.

Evans, R. J. W. *The Wechel Presses*. Oxford: Past and Present, Supplement 2. Oxford, 1975.

Fallières, M. O. and Chanoine Durengues. "Enquête sur les commencements du Protestantisme en Agenais" in *Recueil des travaux de la société d'agriculture d'Agen* 16 (1913): 213–386.

Ferretti, Guiliano. *Un soldat philosophe*. Genoa: E.C.I.G., 1988.

François, Michel. *Le Cardinal de Tournon*. Paris: E. de Boccard,1951.

Galtier, Octave. *Etienne Dolet*. Paris: Flammarion, 1908.

Gardère, J. "Les écoles de Condom," *Revue de Gascogne* 26 (1885): 483.

Gaullieur, Ernest. *Histoire du college de Guyenne*. Paris: Sandoz et Fischbacher, 1879.

Gauna, Max. *Upwellings. First Expressions of Unbelief in the Printed Literature of the French Renaissance*. Rutherford: Fairleigh Dickinson University Press, 1992.

Gay, Peter. *The Enlightenment: An Interpretation*. 2 vols. New York: Knopf, 1967–69.

Goiffon, Abbé. *L'instruction publique à Nîmes*. Nîmes: Grimaud, 1876.

Grafton, Anthony. *Defenders of the Text*. Cambridge: Harvard University Press, 1991.

———. *Joseph Scaliger*. Oxford: Clarendon Press, 1983.

Guggisberg, Hans R. *S. Castellio im Urteil seiner Nachwelt*. Basel: Helbing & Lichtenhahn, 1956.

Hauser, Henri. *Etudes sur la réforme française*. Paris: Picard, 1909.

Hooykaas, R. *Humanisme, Science et Réforme: Pierre de la Ramée (1515–1572)*. Leiden: Brill, 1958.

Hunter, Michael, and David Wootton, eds. *Atheism from the Reformation to the Enlightenment*. Oxford: Oxford University Press, 1996.

Huppert, George. *After the Black Death: A Social History of Early Modern Europe*. Bloomington: Indiana University Press, 1966.

———. "The Age of Philosophy." *EMF: Studies in Early Modern France* 2 (1996): 16–28.

———. "Antiquity Observed: A French Naturalist in the Aegean Sea in 1547," *International Journal of the Classical Tradition* 2:2 (1995): 275–283.

———. "Classes Dangereuses," in *Les Réformes*. Edited by B. Chevalier and R. Sauzet (Tours: 1985), 271–278.

———. "Divinatio et Eruditio," *History and Theory* XIII (1974): 191–207.

———. "The Idea of Civilization in the Sixteenth Century." *Studies in Honor of Hans Baron* (Florence, 1974), 759–769.

———. *The Idea of Perfect History: Historical Erudition and Historical Philosophy in Renaissance France*. Urbana & Chicago: University of Illinois Press, 1970.

———. "La Liberté du cerveau," in *Mélanges en l'honneur de Fernand Braudel* (Toulouse, 1973), II: 267–277.

———. "La rencontre de la philosophie et de l'histoire," in *Le Corpus: Revue de Philosophie* 28 (1995): 11–26.

——. *Les Bourgeois Gentilshommes. An Essay on the Definition of Elites in Renaissance France*. Chicago: University of Chicago Press, 1977.

——. "Lucullus, Crassus and Cato in Grenoble," *Historical Reflections* XV, 1 (1988): 271–278.

——. "Naissance de l'histoire de France," *Annales E.S.C.* (1968): 60–105.

——. "Pasquier Philosophe," in *Etienne Pasquier et ses recherches de la France*. Paris: Presses de l'Ecole Normale Supérieure, 1991.

——. Peter Ramus: The Humanist as Philosophe," *Modern Language Quarterly* 51:2 (Summer 1992): 108–223.

——. *Public Schools in Renaissance France*. Urbana & Chicago: University of Illinois Press, 1984.

——. "The Renaissance Background of Historicism," *History and Theory*, V (1966): 48–60.

——. "Ruined Schools: The End of the Renaissance System of Education in France," in *Humanism in Crisis*, ed. Philippe Desan. Ann Arbor: University of Michigan Press, 1991.

——. "Soziale Mobilität in der Dauphiné im 16. und 17. Jahrhundert," in Winfried Schulze, ed., *Ständische Gesellschaft und Soziale Mobilität. Schriften des Historischen Kollegs*. (Munich: 1988), 179–185.

——. "The Trojan Franks and Their Critics," *Studies in the Renaissance*, XII (1965): 227–241.

Imbart de la Tour, Pierre. *Les origines de la réforme*. 3 vols. Paris: Hachette, 1905–14.

Jehasse, Jean. *La Renaissance de la critique*. St. Etienne: Publications de l'Université de St. Etienne, 1976.

Joy, Lynn Samida. *Gassendi the Atomist*. Cambridge: Cambridge University Press, 1987.

Jurgens, Madeleine, ed. *Ronsard et ses amis*. Paris: Archives Nationales, 1985.

Kelley, Donald. "Louis le Caron Philosophe." In E. P. Mahoney, ed., *Philosophy and Humanism: Renaissance Essays in Honor of P. O. Kristeller*. Leiden: Brill, 1976.

Lachèvre, F. *Le procès du poète Thèophile de Viau*. Paris: Champion, 1909.

Lauvergnat-Gaignère, Christiane. *Lucien de Samosate et le lucianisme en France au 16ᵉᵐᵉ siècle*. Geneva: Droz, 1988.

Leake, Roy. "A. Fouquelin and the Pleïade." *Bibliothèque d'Humanisme et Renaissance*, 32 (1970): 379–394.

Le Coultre, Jean Jules. *Mathurin Cordier et les origines de la pedagogie protestante dans les pays de langue française (1530–1564)*. Neuchâtel: Secretariat de l'Université, 1926.

Leibacher-Ouvrard, Lise. *Libertinage et utopies sous le règne de Louis XIV*. Geneva: Droz, 1989.

Lestringant, Frank. *André Thevet*. Geneva: Droz, 1991.

Lienhard, Marc, ed. *Croyants et sceptiques au seizième siècle*. Strasbourg: Librairie ISTRA, 1981.

Magne, Emile. *Ninon de Lanclos*. London: Arrowsmith, 1926.

McFarlane, I. D. *Buchanan*. London: Duckworth, 1981.

Ménard, Léon. *Histoire de Nîmes*. 7 vols. Paris: H. D. Chaubert, 1744–1758.

Menk, Gerhard. *Die Hohe Schule Herborn*. Wiesbaden: Selbstverlag der Historischen Kommission für Nassau, 1981.

Mortier, Roland. *Clartés et Ombres du siècle des lumières*. Geneva: Droz, 1969.

Moss, Ann. *Printed Commonplace Books and the Structure of Renaissance Thought*. Oxford: Clarendon Press, 1996.

Niderst, Alain. *Fontenelle à la recherche de lui-même (1657–1702)*. Paris: Nizet, 1972.

Nolhac, Pierre de. *Ronsard et l'humanisme*. Paris: Champion, 1921.

Ong, W. J. *Ramus and the Decline of Rhetoric*. Cambridge: Harvard University Press, 1958.

Peach, Trevor. *Nature et Raison. Etude critique des Dialogues de Jacques Tahureau*. Geneva: Slatkine, 1986.

Pérouse, G. A., ed. *Etudes sur E. Dolet.* Geneva: Droz, 1993.

Perrin, Nicole. "La vie religieuse," in *Le curé Meslier.* Reims: Bibliothèque de l'Université de Reims, 1980.

Pintard, René. *Le libertinage érudit.* Paris: Slatkine, 1983.

Pinvert, Lucien. *Lazare de Baïf.* Paris: A. Fontemoing, 1900.

Popkin, Richard and Charles B. Schmitt, eds. *Scepticism from the Renaissance to the Enlightenment.* Wiesbaden: Harassowitz, 1987.

Potez, Henri. "Deux années de le Renaissance." *Revue d'histoire littéraire de la France* 13 (1906): 458–498; 658–692.

———. "La jeunesse de Denys Lambin." *Revue de l'histoire littéraire de la France* 9 (1902): 385–413.

Prudhomme, A. "L'enseignement secondaire à Grenoble," *Bulletin de l'Academie Delphinale* 14 (1900): 93–139.

Rétat, Pierre. *Le dictionnaire de Bayle et la lutte philosophique au 18ᵉᵐᵉ siècle.* Paris: Les Belles Lettres, 1971.

Rice, Eugene F., Jr. *The Renaissance Idea of Wisdom.* Cambridge: Harvard University Press, 1958.

Rosenberg, Aubrey. *Tyssot de Patot.* The Hague: Nijhoff, 1972.

Sabrié, J. B. *Pierre Charron.* Paris: F. Alcan, 1913.

Schmitt, Charles B. *The Aristotelian Tradition and Renaissance Universities.* London: Variorum Reprints, 1984.

———. *Cicero Scepticus.* The Hague: Nijhoff, 1972.

Screech, M. A. *Rabelais.* Ithaca: Cornell University Press, 1979.

Sharrat, Peter. "N. Nancelius, Petri Rami Vita." *Humanistica Lovanensia*, XXIV (1975).

Spink, J. S. *French Freethought from Gassendi to Voltaire.* London: Athlone Press, 1960.

Strauss, Leo. *La persécution et l'art d'écrire.* Paris: Livre de Poche, 1989.

Sturel, René. *Jacques Amyot.* Paris: Champion, 1908.

Tamizey de Larroque, Ph. *Essai sur la vie et les ouvrages de Florimond de Raymond.* Paris: A. Aubry, 1867.

Trinquet, Roger. *La jeunesse de Montaigne.* Paris: Nizet, 1972.

Vernière, Paul. *Spinoza.* 2 vols. Paris: P.U.F., 1954.

Waddington, Charles. *Ramus.* Paris: C. Meyrueis, 1855.

Weber, Henri. "Meslier et le 16ᵉᵐᵉ siècle, in *Etudes sur Meslier.* Paris: Société des Études Robespierristes, 1966.

Whitmore, P. J. S. *The Order of Minims in Seventeenth-Century France.* The Hague: Nijoff, 1967.

Yardeni, Miriam. *Utopie et révolte sous Louis XIV.* Paris: Nizet, 1980.

Zanta, Léontine. *La Renaissance du Stoïcisme au 16ᵉᵐᵉ siècle.* Paris: Champion 1914.

Zingler, Ilana. "Narration et Témoignage dans les Observations de Pierre Belon." *Nouvelle Revue du Seizième Siècle* 5 (1987): 25–40.

INDEX

George Huppert is Professor of
History at the University of Illinois at Chicago.
He is author of *The Idea of Perfect History: Historical
Erudition and Historical Philosophy in Renaissance France,
Les Bourgeois Gentilhommes: An Essay on the Definition of
Elites in Renaissance France, Public Schools in Renaissance
France,* and *After the Black Death: A Social
History of Modern Europe.*